DARKER

TEACHINGS OF
THE IMMORTALS

BY
MIKAL NYGHT

☥

*Are you **sure**
you want to live forever?*

Darker Teachings of the Immortals
Author: Mikal Nyght
Publisher: Eye Scry Publications
www.eyescrypublications.com
Copyright © 2017
All rights reserved

ISBN: 978-1-942415-15-2

WHOLESALE INFORMATION

For information about wholesale rates,
or to order additional copies, please email us at...

info@eyescrypublications.com

Visit the author's website at

www.immortalis-animus.com

Dedication

Love is the reason...
the *only* reason for any of it.

And so this book is for The One
who brought me to Life
and showed me the way.

The core of your beliefs
determines the realities you *see*
and obliterates those
you choose to ignore.

Introduction
Life Gets In the Way

The observation has been made that "life gets in the way," and while that's true, it's really something more specific that lies at the heart of our conundrum. Namely – life gets in the way of *immortality*.

Ironic, no?

While one is off doing all the things one does in the course of living, life is being drained out of you by the brute with the scythe, until you wake up one morning and realize you are old, wondering where your life went, what became of time, and why the reflection in the mirror bears no resemblance to the idea of yourself in your mind.

So, yes, life gets in the way. It is not my belief that one should live as an isolated monk in a state of perpetual meditation and contemplation of one's navel. Is that really living? On the other hand, I have lived in simpler times – before man walked on the moon, before the age of the internet, before X-Box and blue tooth and smart phones and all the other distractions the world now has to offer. Perhaps I sound like an old man. I am. I am a *very* old man, in a very transient world.

What does that mean? What does that have to do with the price of coffee, you ask? Nothing. And everything.

What it means is that I have not only seen the world change, I have seen *people* change. I have seen their attention shift from self to family to community to global to universal. And yet, is that really the direction in which one wants to be moving?

What? Is Mikal saying we should be entirely myopic, only focused on the Self? Yes. And no. And yes. A primary aspect of *The Darker Teachings* is that *you* are the core and heart of the universe, despite what you have been taught to believe by well-meaning grandmas and religious fanatics. Nowadays, the world offers so many causes and so much information that the brain/mind becomes overloaded and waterlogged with what you are *told* is important, but which you can really do nothing about in the big picture, regardless of your good-intentioned (but most often false) belief systems.

You cannot be free for as long as you are energetically chained to others – whether family, friends or strangers in distant lands. With that said – no, I am not suggesting one should break all ties and go live in a commune. No, I do not have any interest in separating seekers from their foundations in order to start a cult, despite occasional accusations. Cults are high maintenance and far more trouble than they could ever be worth, or so I hear. Cults generally do not end well. Ask David Koresh[1] or Jim Jones[2]. You can't, of course. They're both dead. But there are plenty of functioning cults right here, right now, right in front of you. Start with the Catholic Church and work your way down from there, since a cult is any organization that depends on false beliefs spoon-fed to its followers, usually delivering threats of pain and death. Or eternal damnation, hellfire and brimstone. Sound about right?

But no matter. That's another dark teaching for another dark night of the soul.

---

[1] David Koresh was the American leader of the Branch Davidians religious sect, believing himself to be its final prophet. Koresh allegedly died when his compound was burned to the ground by the US government.

[2] James Warren Jones (May 13, 1931 - November 18, 1978) was an American cult leader and communist. Jones was ordained as a Disciples of Christ pastor, and achieved notoriety as the founder and leader of the radical leftist Peoples Temple, which was often described as having cult-like qualities. It has been debated for decades as to whether Jim Jones drank the suicide Kool-Aid or not.

What I *am* saying is that one has to have a keen awareness. Anything that doesn't augment one's life is essentially *taking* one's life, slowly but surely. Think about it. Without Awareness with a capital A you will find yourself drained of all your lifeforce sooner than you think. The energy vampires are all around you – on the internet, in your schools and places of work, in your family, and even in your circle of friends.

You can't change the world.
You can only change yourself.

If the world changes as a result of the changes you bring about in yourself, it will be a shift of your own perception, not a shift of reality as it is commonly understood. That's good – by changing yourself, you *do* change the world in that you change your view of it, and therefore your experience of it.

You can't change other people.
You can only change yourself.

If other people seem to change as a result of what you learn and experience on your path, it will be because the changes you have brought about in *yourself* elicit different reactions and different outcomes in the people around you. That's good. By changing yourself, you *do* change other people in the sense that you empower them. You can hand them the tools, but you can't even teach them how to use those tools if they don't want to learn. And believe me – most don't. They want to dally at the edge of the pond, but they don't really want to get wet by throwing themselves into the deep end. They are not your responsibility. *Period.*

> *You won't find immortality or any other form of*
> *spiritual evolution within the 3-Ds*

What are the 3-Ds? Diversion, distraction, dissipation. It's one thing to watch tv for an hour or log on to the internet and surf for a little while. It's another matter altogether when it becomes your entire existence, when you lose sleep wondering what so-and-so said about you on such-and-such a blog or Facebook group. What other people think of you is none of your business. Hard lesson, but an important one. What you think of them is none of their business, so don't waste time rattling your cyber-saber in some deep-seated need to be right.

There is no right.

There is no wrong.

There is only perception.

And for that matter, what do you get if you *are* right? There are no gold stars on this path. There are no kudos attached to your profile. There is only yourself and your Other, your energetic twin[3], and somewhere in the middle is the narrow way that leads from organic to inorganic, from mortal to immortal.

Many times over the years I've been asked, "What's the real purpose of *The Darker Teachings*?" This question tends to come up when it is observed that I don't really offer a series of techniques or exercises conveniently designed to instill or install the immortal condition into those who choose to travel this path. The simple reality of it is that there are no specific practices or exercises one can do to grasp immortality. There is only Intent, action and (eventually) manifestation.

Therefore, the purpose of *The Darker Teachings* is primarily to generate and hopefully *maintain* a frame of mind of freedom from the programming that otherwise binds the

---

[3] The twin (or Other) is the totality of oneself, but can be visualized as the energetic vessel into which the seeker uploads his consciousness through the process of self-creation. The Other is the energy body personified and occasionally even manifested in ordinary awareness, developed to a point of extreme cohesion through Intent and Dreaming. It may take on a life of its own, and is the core source of what humans commonly misconstrue as "past lives."

seeker to mortality, death and decay. The purpose is to teach the seeker not *what* to think, but *how* to think and – far more importantly – how to *see* that the world is largely an illusion of delusions, created and nurtured by fear, complacency and habit.

Am I saying the world isn't real? Not at all. It is *very* real, and as paranoid as this might sound, it really *is* out to get you – not through ninja assassins or shadowy entities looking to steal your soul, but through absorption into the dull and lifeless status quo of so-called normal life.

You *will* be absorbed if you don't do something. *Teachings of the Immortals* was designed to provide the seekers for whom it was written with an intense and compelling Awakening. *The Darker Teachings* are intended to move the traditional reference points from the ordinary to the infinite, from the transient to the eternal. Though some have described *Teachings of the Immortals* as poetic, lyrical and sensually alluring, it is sometimes necessary to speak in cold and concise terms, without poetry or literary dalliance, but with the grim, graceless, and gut-wrenching voice of the ugly truth, which is another aspect of *The Darker Teachings*.

The Darker Teachings are for tearing away the blinders and comfort zones and replacing them with an ever-present awareness that transcends the humanform and brings the seeker ever closer to the actualization of the immortal condition.

But make no mistake: it's not just the internet and the smart phones and the video games and all the rest of Agent Smith's tools that have the power to thwart your Intent. It's the world as a whole, which has become increasingly complex. I come from a time when play and entertainment hailed from imagination and invention. One was required to create his own fantasy worlds and people them with the characters from his mind's eye. Now, that is all but a lost art – yet it really is *the* key to creating and manifesting the Other. Without imagination and a real passion for the dreams that can be found only in your own heart, the Other withers and dies for lack of energy, for lack of creative inspiration, for lack of love. The Other dies from the disease of the 3-Ds.

Why am I telling you these things? Only because I am keenly aware of the world in which we all live – and I can tell you with absolute certainty that it was probably easier 20 years ago, or 50 years ago, or 100 years ago than it is now, to achieve the immortal condition. Why? Because the matrix re-designs itself every moment in an attempt to obstruct seekers. Evolution is not a birthright. It is a monumental *task* – "The Great Work" of a lifetime. The Agent Smith of a hundred years ago is not the same as the Agent Smith of today. The matrix learns and grows, and will throw everything in its power at you to keep you from completing your journey.

What to do? It's up to you. Everything begins with a thought, and every thought results in a choice.

Make the impeccable choice whenever possible.

And know this: it is *always* possible. When you forget that, you have become just another phantom[4] on the road to death.

Create yourself with passion, with imagination, and with unconditional love. Anything less is a crime against yourself.

Many of the entries in this volume of *The Darker Teachings* have been gleaned from my online forum, Immortal Spirit, which has been in operation since 2010. It is often the questions posed by those on a path of self-discovery that enable me to tap into the deepest veins of silent knowing, the darkest blood of the sentient but predatory universe. It is also from these questions that we get a clearer picture of the seekers themselves – the questions and concerns generated by virtue of living in today's chaotic world.

---

[4] Phantom: individuals still plugged into the beliefs of the consensual reality. Phantoms define themselves by what they do, the company they keep, the church they attend, their social status. Another mark of a phantom is that they possess an unlimited number of personalities and roles, all without the cohesion of a single, unified "I-Am". Phantoms are organic machines within the larger machine.

And so I would tell you: always ask the next question and be open to the answers you might least expect, even when they are not what you *want* to hear, but are always in tune with what you *need* to hear.

> *"If you read the darker teachings before you are ready, you may end up holding a candlelight vigil for your sanity."*
> **– Jonathan Abrahms, Independent Reviewer**

What this advance reviewer had to say is a dark truth unto itself. *The Darker Teachings* must be approached cautiously, with respect, and only when you are ready to abandon what you presently believe in order to embrace an eternal mindset as opposed to your currently transient existence.

The Darker Teachings are intentionally not presented in any straightforward, linear, logical manner. Many will appear to be repetitive – and indeed, they are. The reasons for this are many, but the bottom line is that only when the mind can be unplugged from its traditional neural pathways does it become possible to perceive above and beyond what you have already been programmed to believe. I refer to this form of communication as mind-tongue or heart-tongue – the scenic bypass off the main roads.

Therefore, I would advise...

Listen with your heart.
Hear with your spirit.
See with your third eye.
Only then will you Know.

This is meant literally.
You are not what you Think you are.

- Mikal Nyght
October 2017

11

The Darker Teachings

Why Are The Darker Teachings Dangerous?

You once said that the darker teachings can be harmful, up to and including the possibility of madness. What – exactly – did you mean by that? Enlightened yoga masters in India regularly appear totally mad to normal people.

If you put one sane man in a room full of madmen, that man will appear irrefutably mad.

The knowledge offered in *Teachings of the Immortals*, on my website, and in this current volume can and will change you at a fundamental level if you let them. Since sanity is judged by a consensus of what is considered normal within a given percentage of society, anyone who is outside the parameters of the consensus will be deemed mad. It matters not in the least that this madness is actually sanity, and those generally considered sane in today's world are really mad as any shithouse mouse. What matters is that if you are thought to be insane within their consensus, you are at the mercy of their judgments, laws and punishments.

Tread carefully.

In addition, there is a very real possibility that the darker teachings themselves *can* drive someone mad – but *only* if the seeker is unwilling or unable to release his hold on the belief systems of his existing programs. In other words – you can't have it both ways. If you try, it becomes rather like a scene out of an old episode of *Star Trek*, wherein Captain Kirk drives a computer to self-destruct by feeding it conflicting truths.

Kirk (speaking to a computer): "I'm telling you the truth."
Harry Mudd: "Everything Kirk says is a lie."

The resulting conflict ends in madness because the contradiction is fundamental and therefore *cannot* be resolved. He's telling the truth, but everything he says is a lie. Trying to hold onto one's dayshine beliefs while simultaneously opening to the teachings can have dangerous and potentially irreversible consequences. Again, tread carefully and enter here only when you are ready to make the commitment to the eternal self as opposed to holding onto the false identity of the dayshine persona.

In candles and cobwebs
we see the hex
of our mortality.

One is the Loneliest Number

What every seeker needs to know going in is that very few ever come out on the other side. There are some (very few) who are compelled to do this thing. One might say you have the hunger for the unknown already in your blood - the love affair with the mystical, and an almost unnatural disdain for the mortal world and all its mundane manifestations.

This is why I tell you, *"You are The One."*

Even if you enter into this journey with friends or life-long companions, most of them will slowly but inevitably drift away until you find yourself alone on the side of a mountain in a blizzard, with only your own wits upon which to depend. And while this can be frustrating and even deeply hurtful, it isn't at all uncommon. Even so, it isn't their fault, and certainly not yours. Very few (less than 1% of 1% of the human population) are actually compelled to do this thing that is said to be impossible. And of that 1% of 1%, fewer than 1% of those will actually succeed in *Doing* it.

The fact that you find yourself alone is a good omen, all things considered. You have given yourself that minuscule window of opportunity.

It isn't necessary to get a divorce or banish your friends to some lost branch of Lethe. They are human. What matters is whether you can do this thing alone. Most can't. Those who do quickly discover what is meant by my statement, *'The path will cost you everything.'*

The One means simply that.

One.

One is the loneliest number.

I am the shadow's shadow,
snowfrost melting on elm arms,
rain on the River Styx.

From the left tributary of Lethe,
my reflection stares up at me
fanged fiend
woven of moon kisses
and immortal wishes.

I blink.
The mirror is empty.

Shadow me runs free,
beyond the reach
of pallid dawn,
beyond the dream
of Time.

Transcendence vs. Transmogrification

What determines whether a seeker achieves transmogrification, or whether they transcend at the moment of mortal death?

Near as I can figure on all my fingers and toes, it is a quantum leap of sorts. Even if two seekers at the same point in their journey have the exact same knowledge and information, one might suddenly have that quantum leap of understanding, while the other – equally advanced in all ways – never does. It is not something that can be predicted, but it is precisely why unbending and ruthless attention must be given to the equation at all times. I don't mean a 24/7 application of thought toward the equation, but a 24/7 *awareness* of its intent, woven into the fabric of self and Other. Here words fail. It is possible to focus on something even when doing other things. It is possible to dream the intent even if not in direct dreamings.

The quantum leap which instigates transmogrification is rare, but not at all impossible. *Allow the impossible.* There is a lot to be said for that – an unwritten integer in the equation – Intent + Action = Manifestation. I have wondered if the reason some seekers fail to transmogrify (but embrace transcendence) is because they do not possess the ability to allow the impossible. They may very well believe in the *idea* of transmogrification, but they may also be running background programs which are telling them, "Sure, it's a great idea, but I'm not worthy and my genes are wrong and my hair isn't the right color and it's dark on Tuesday, so it ain't gonna happen to *me*." Whatever the program, whether religious or social or just cultural, those belief systems not yet eradicated can and will plug up even the most determined assholes, particularly if one is not aware of the mental and spiritual constipation.

Ultimately, it really does appear to be a quantum leap which some can make and others never do. And there is no rhyme or reason to it that I can accurately determine. And this is another reason this has been largely housed under the roof of *The Darker Teachings*. Some things have no definitive answer, which makes them all the more intriguing, but also all the more frustrating, no?

Of Kwai Chang Cain and Dust
A look at synchronicity

I now understand why the loneliness on this path is so prevalent. One must build the foundation and do the work alone, very much like David Carradine's character in the old Kung Fu *television series.*

I pay special attention when unlikely coincidences poke out of the fabric of the quantum universe to taunt me. Just before logging on to the forum this morning, I was reading a comment on another site. In it, the statement was made, "I think a real warrior can *be* a warrior in any environment – rather like Kwai Chang Cain walking through the world as Himself whether in the monastery or the real world. It's who we are inside that determines how we will meet the path."

When unlikely synchronicities such as this occur, I stop and ask myself, in this case, "What is the significance of Kwai Chang Cain? What does the character represent that has significance to me at this point in time?" The answer may not always be clear at first, but it is important to acknowledge the synchronicity as validation that the world is nothing like one has been taught to believe, evidence that the quantum gears of the Otherworld are spinning and turning in the shadows of our own creation.

Yesterday, I was looking back on some old commentary I had made on another website, wherein I had said, "My television gathers dust in the corner while lazy mice nibble the pages of very old books." As I was reading this, a friend who is visiting entered the room and made the observation: "Your tv is covered with dust. Would you like me to clean it for you?"

These are the types of synchronicities that validate and confirm that the universe is an interactive game of self-creation. And a trickster with an unusual sense of humor.

You will go mad as a spider monkey feeding on crack-covered espresso beans. You start telling relatives that your new chosen path is a quest for immortality, and they are going to have you put away. It's easy to see why this knowledge has been hidden and shrouded for so many thousands of years.

If you are familiar with the works of Carlos Castaneda, there is a concept in one of his books that became extremely unpopular and controversial, but which is nonetheless imbued with absolute truth. It is this:

I think everything boils down to one act: you must leave your friends. You must say good-bye to them, for good. It's not possible for you to continue on the warrior's path carrying your personal history with you, and unless you discontinue your way of life, I won't be able to go ahead with my instruction.

Your friends are your family, they are your points of reference. Therefore, they have to go. Sorcerers have only one point of reference: infinity.

You must simply leave, leave any way you can.

You have never been alone in your life. This is the time to do it. I don't want your body to die physically. I want your *person* to die. The two are very different affairs. In essence, your person has very little to do with your body. Your person is your mind, and believe you me, your mind is not yours.

I'll tell you about that subject someday, but not while you're cushioned by your friends.

The criteria that indicates that a sorcerer is dead is when it makes no difference to him whether he has company or whether he is alone. The day you don't covet the company of your friends, whom you use as shields, that's the day that your person has died.

– Don Juan to Carlos Castaneda
The Active Side of Infinity

While these words were uttered by an old Mexican shaman, they have relevance here as well. In most cases, unless one's friends are also seekers, they are phantoms, through and through. There is no middle ground. That being the case, you really don't have the luxury of telling friends and family what you are doing or what you are pursuing. The agenda of phantoms is the same as the agenda of Agent Smith. Only when you know that and live by it will you have any chance of manifesting your Intent.

The problem most seekers encounter is that they don't know the difference between their "person" and the authentic Self. The person is the masks and roles one takes on *without awareness* – it's the reason that when an adult child goes to visit her mother, the daughter's voice goes up an octave, and she starts behaving like a little girl because that is the role she has always inhabited with her mother. So when don Juan says "your person must die," it's important to know what is meant by the word "person." I prefer to use the term "false identity" or "actor".

Has your actor died or is she alive and well and acting in the role of Agent Smith without your even knowing it? What steps have you taken to destroy your false identities?

It's interesting to note that if you hear your internal dialog kick in when considering the idea of releasing those false identities (*"Harrumph and how-do-you-do, we don't have to listen to this crap!" "Burn that book and fuck that bastard!" "Boil that dust speck! Boil that dust speck!"*), chances are your person is the man behind the curtain shouting in your ear while the brute with the scythe stalks you from the shadows.

All In the Family?

I have this idea about "family" that I'm starting to question. Seems like my family expects me to be there when they need me, but they really aren't there when I need them. To what extent does a seeker owe allegiance to his biological family?

A true seeker owes allegiance to no one other than himself – an unpopular opinion, but also a darker truth few want to examine. In reality, the family unit has become somewhat obsolete. In the past, it was necessary to have a functioning unit to insure the survival and relative safety of all its members – but with that unit came a structure that evolved into a paradigm that can be tremendously restrictive and limiting – not to mention the paradigm is in complete service to the program itself. Why? Because it requires adopting roles and adhering to them "for the good of all" rather than for the evolution of the individual members of the family.

The Man of the House was charged with the responsibility of providing food and shelter (even if he might not be altogether suited to the task emotionally or physically). The Lady of the House was saddled with the expectation of bearing and raising children (even if she might not be suited to the task emotionally or physically). The children were expected to be seen and not heard, while simultaneously being raised as field hands or heirs to the throne, depending on the social and economical status of the family as a whole. All family members were expected to toe the line with regard to communal beliefs – religion, politics, morals – and those who didn't found themselves excommunicated in one way or another, even if only in being emotionally shunned by other family members with whom they might not see eye to eye.

20

The result of this type of corralling is that the program thrives while those supporting it (even if unwittingly) tend to wither on the vine as a byproduct of trying to serve the needs of the many by ignoring the needs of The One. The mold into which one finds oneself shoved becomes so confining that one either succumbs to the pressures and expectations of the family, or packs one's hobo sack and heads for the sanctuary of the hills before being consumed utterly.

But aren't we communal creatures by nature? Isn't it written somewhere in our DNA that we actually need a family?

It's really only written in the small print of The Program. Beyond a certain point, humans are largely self-sufficient. I'll confine my comments here to adults rather than children – since clearly it is necessary for some manner of caregiver in the first few months or even the first few years of life. But as an adut, do you *need* a family, or do you just like the *idea* of one? And is that idea realistic, or only rooted in some 1950s tv sitcom?

You mentioned that your family seems to need you but is seldom there when the reverse is true. You might want to stop and look at that and what it ultimately means. Are you bound to your family out of love, or only out of a sense of duty and obligation? And are you bound to them because they share your blood (nothing more than a biological accident) or because they share even some small percentage of your philosophies of Life? (It may surprise you to discover that *most* family members have little in common when all is said and done).

I once knew a seeker who argued vehemently for her love of family – in this case, a doting mother and father who kept her well-supplied with houses, automobiles, and all manner of material possessions. She never worked a day in her life and never wanted for anything, and to her this translated to the notion that she was deeply loved. The reality, of course, was a bit different. While the parents may well have loved her in an emotional sense, they also recognized that they had created a monster who had become *incapable* of survival in the real world, and so it was a sense of obligation on their part that imbued them with the need to feed the monster lest it descend on the village and devour the unsuspecting peasants.

It wasn't love that kept the wheels turning. It was self-preservation on the part of the parents, and complete lack of personal responsibility on the part of the child. Put simply: codependency taken to the nth degree of codependency.

What this seeker didn't realize was that the expectations placed onto her as a result would eventually destroy her ability to *be* a seeker at all. She found herself conflicted, and eventually abandoned the path altogether – not out of ideological differences with her parents (though they were legion), but because she could not bear to give up the *illusion* of a loving family. So she put the mask back on, wears the happy grin of a phantom, and goes through the motions of it all while making frequent visits to her therapist's expensively padded couch.

While there might be exceptions (and you are all free to adopt the illusion that *your* family is the exception), it is generally true that families serve the unit far more than any individual within that unit.

> *So what do you consider to be a family, Mikal? Is there such a thing anymore?*

My father is the old man at the train station who speaks in tongues and walks with a pronounced limp. My grandmother is the spider suspended in her web, content with all the Nothing she owns. My children are stray kittens lost in the storm, and the cricket singing from his earthen crib.

Family is who you choose and those who choose you in return. It has nothing to do with the blood running through your veins or some name that may stretch back to the days before Jesus was a twinkle in the eye of a blind god. It has to do with unity of purpose, shared life experience, and, most of all, the unconditional love you feel for someone you recognize as a kindred spirit.

Just for the record, lest those little voices pipe up and accuse me of trying to subvert the family unit (*"Do you think he's onto us? Quick – get the duct tape and let's shut him up for good!"*) I do concede that there are times when a *functioning* family unit can have its advantages, and as cold as this may sound, it's always up to the individual to consider this question: *Is the price too high?*

It's one thing to sacrifice a few hours of your time (though when it becomes a habit is when it becomes dangerous). It's another thing altogether when you are asked to sacrifice who you *are* in order to maintain your standing in The Family. If you find yourself having to uphold a lot of false beliefs and even lies, you might want to consider whether you are in a family or a prison or even a cult. (Yes, these are called "The Darker Teachings" for a reason.)

Love is the Reason

This segment appears in *Teachings of the Immortals*, but is sufficiently relevant to warrant inclusion here as foundational information. Without wholly embracing the idea that 'Love is the Reason,' the seeker is destined to fail.

> *When you love something so much that you cannot envision a world in which your love is dead, that is the first moment you might begin to see the pathway to achieving the immortal condition. That is the moment you might even understand why it is a compulsion for you and not just a passing intellectual dalliance.*

I've highlighted the paragraph above because it is really all that matters here, distilled down to 57 words or less. If you get it, you're already ahead of the game, but don't fool yourself by thinking, *"Well, duh, that's obvious, Mikal!"* Yes, it's obvious, but so is that oncoming bus, and people walk in front of buses every day.

The secret here is that you have to create and inhabit a world where Death himself does not and *cannot* exist, for another fundamental truth is that only when you evolve sufficiently to be beyond the reach of Death does it become possible to also envision the immortal condition – not only for yourself, but also with regard to those you love.

Does this mean you can save them from Death? No. And yes. And no. What it means is that in order to even begin to comprehend the meaning of this statement, you would need to be already standing on the far side of the bridge between life and death, looking back to see how the bridge was built. It is not something that can be explained with words or pictures drawn in the sands of time. It is something that can be intuited at first, so I hope you will tickle the riddle rather than struggling to pick it apart. For now, I will simply say this: *in a world where Death does not exist for the One, Death does not exist at All.*

Perhaps I have said too much.

Whether the thing you love is another human being, or the thought of your eternal Other, or simply the idea of Being *alive*, rest assured that the kind of love that is transformative is not love of a physical object or even another person, place or thing.

What? You just contradicted yourself!

Yes, I did.

Or did I?

When I am speaking of love at this level, I am not talking about the *form* in which the object of one's love appears, but the *essence* within the form itself. The *energy* of it. The *spirit* of it. The sheer and inexplicable *awe* of it. To an immortal, a

24

lover's form may appear as an old woman, haggish and withered, but the *essence* of the lover is no less vibrant and alive than on the day they met. The essence is that which is eternal, and therefore it is the fundamental nature which the seeker truly loves, rather than the transient form.

Love of the immortal Other is a barometer for some, while others would say the twin is merely a reflection of the self. Listen to your internal dialog, because if it is telling you that your twin is "*only*" this or that, if those pesky little voices are telling you the twin is "*only*" the so-called higher self or the soul to which you may feel entitled, *think again.*

The Other is the *totality* of oneself, the cumulative experience of all lifetimes, past, present and future. It is not some ethereal or angelic woo-woo hanging in orbit over Uranus, but instead *it is the vessel for the seeker's awareness beyond this life.* Underestimate it at your own peril. Ignore it at the certainty of your obliteration.

Love it... and it will come to you in dreams and visions, it will speak to you through silent knowing (gnosis[5]), it will even infiltrate the past in ways you cannot begin to wrap your mind around until you think it has been with you all along (and it has, once you as the mortal self create it in the Now); and ultimately it will become your best friend, perfect lover, eternal guardian, and temple of the singularity of consciousness[6] which you are in the process of becoming.

---

[5] Gnosis: Silent knowing; communication with the Other and the sentient universe. An altered state of consciousness accessible through simple Intent, meditation, certain mind-altering plant allies, tantric sex, the near-death-experience, sensory deprivation, and many other methods. Over time, as abilities and awareness increase, seekers might come to have a permanent channel to gnosis through the connection to the Other. Achieving that state is one of the seeker's greatest tasks.

[6] Singularity of Consciousness: The self made Whole, the evolution of consciousness which results in a cohesive field of awareness existing ubiquitously and non-locally. The immortal condition. The cohesive, fully integrated *I-Am* consisting of all components of the mortal self and the eternal Other, brought together under a single assemblage point. The individuated totality of oneself, consisting of all (so-called) past lives, future lives and parallel lives.

The real key to attaining the immortal condition is contained within this peculiar force humans call love. And yet, I would urge great caution here, for it is the erroneous conclusions and misconceptions humans have about love that will also prevent them from attaining that state. Be always aware of every thought and every belief system, and always stop and take a moment to ask yourself, "What do I believe about love and why do I believe it?"

There is such a wide range of experience associated with love, it's unfortunate that other words have not been invented to more clearly distinguish between romantic love, sexual love, parental love, familial love, spiritual love, emotional love, the creative force of love, unconditional love, and so on. The word love is used for all of these states, and many more, so it's important for the seeker to have a firm grasp on his own understanding of what I have come to call *the creative force of love.*

This form of love is a quantifiable *force*, not a passive romantic emotion, but a viable power similar in nature to a bolt of lightning, possessing the ability to destroy and create in a single strike.

And yet, words are only descriptions, tools to be used to aid the processes, but not to be mistaken for the process itself. As the old saying goes, do not mistake the finger pointing at the moon for the moon itself.

What does this have to do with the key to attaining the immortal condition? Nothing. And everything.

It is only when the seeker begins to truly experience the *creative* force of love that she will have even the vaguest idea of what the immortal condition actually is, and why one is compelled to attain it. It isn't just the prospect of living forever. That's really quite a daunting thought when you boil it down. Why? Because a linear experience of eternity would consist of boredom and eventual madness, largely because the brain/mind is not designed to process such vast amounts of data as would accumulate from an extremely long and linear

26

organic life. The love I am speaking of here is the love that is devastating in its intensity for it is only when the world is destroyed that the new world can be built in its place.

Love is the reason.

In clinical word-association tests, humans most commonly reply with opposites. If I say "dark," the first and most common response will be "light". Boy/girl. Life/Death. Good/Evil. That being the case, it stands to reason that if I say "love," the most common response will be "hate."

And therein lies a clue to why most humans never even search for the immortal condition.

Somewhere along the way, the human program got even more fucked up than it already was. Somewhere in the depths of the human paradigm, hate came to be considered the opposite of love, when it is crystal clear to anyone outside the program that *grief* is the polar opposite of love.

Grief is the state of loss wherein the object and the essence of what one loves has been eliminated, permanently and irrevocably removed from the fabric of existence. It is the state wherein one realizes that the things one loves (including and especially Oneself) comprise the elements of the answer to the first question: Who Are You?

This is not to say that you are defined by the ones you love. And yet, the essence of who you are is interwoven with the energetic fabric of the essence of the things you love. This is the creative force of love, the catalytic element which causes the seeker to ultimately realize that *without* those things she is left in a state of grief that can debilitate the spirit and even crush the will to live.

To those who would argue that love is therefore an attachment, I would say instead that love is an enhancement, an enrichment, an augmentation. To those who would say that love is a dependency, I would say instead that it is the ultimate freedom, for within the creative force of love lies The Reason, which is the catalyst of all change and evolution.

These are only words tacked to the door of the infinite, hanging somewhere in the wasteland of mindspace. If it were possible to truly define the key to the immortal condition, someone would have done it by now. I have no delusions that I will change the world, alter your perceptions, or even make a dent in the human condition. And yet, what can be *seen* so clearly is often that which defies explanation utterly.

In the life of every true seeker, there is the capacity to love something so fiercely that the element of love becomes a duality[7]. In the same way light is both particle and wave, love is both the experience and the *catalyst* for the experience itself.

> *My only problem is how to carry that singularity of intense realization into my every waking moment. I don't want to realize it once and then have that feeling fade away. Why must the truth of it all be buried so deep inside that it takes an autopsy to dig it out?*

What you realize today is with you always, even if you forget it. The universe is holographic, and therefore all things that have ever happened to you, or ever will happen, are already stored with the hologram that is You. An apprentice once asked me, "What if I figure it out tomorrow, then develop Alzheimer's and forget everything I ever learned?"

While that is a possibility within the dayshine world, the hologram contains every shred of all your experience throughout the space-time continuum. Therefore, even if you were to forget what you've learned, it's still there within the hologram, part of who you *are*.

Nothing is ever truly lost.

---

[7] Duality: Duality (as opposed to dualism) allows for two seemingly contradictory conditions to exist simultaneously, without either obliterating or in any way usurping the other. Example: "a love/hate relationship". Another example: We exist as mortal human beings in the Now, and simultaneously as eternal beings through the energy body of the Other. Duality can be studied in the statement, "You must *be* immortal before you will know how to *become* immortal."

The Politics of the Path
An Immortal's Perspective in the Form of a Rant

If you are caught in the leg trap of religion or the cesspool of politics, then you have not yet overcome the part of you that thinks "It Matters!"

When a seeker tells me, "I like to be informed," what I am really hearing is the prittle-prattle of self-importance and the puffing out of the chest which indicates that the seeker has become so full of shit that he cannot see the forest for the big brown logs he is producing to obscure his own path.

"Oh my precious frilly lord!" some are certain to exclaim. *"Is Mikal saying we shouldn't vote? shouldn't care? shouldn't even know what's going on in the world?"* No. What I'm saying is that a true seeker doesn't need to get involved in the political monkey circus unless he has made the *commitment* to the consensus, and if that is the case, then he might as well abandon this path altogether, suckle up to the sweet teat of Society, become a card-carrying member of The Real World, and therefore also a member in good standing of The Lunatic Majority, which would try to convince you of its righteous goodness by virtue of its numbers and all those celebrities with their perfectly capped white teeth who smile the alluring smile of a phantom and tell you why you should vote for This or That Trending Asshole, when the reality is that you already know right from wrong in your tiny little heart if you have even the slightest glint of awareness somewhere in that confuzzled orb sitting on the top of your shoulders.

Ah, but now the wicked vampire king has only confuzzled you all the more, no?

No. Yes. Maybe.

Within every living creature (and most inorganics) there is a frequency that aligns with silent knowing. Put simply, you already know through your own intuitive awareness who or what to vote for (if you must insist on playing such pedantic games), you already know who and where The One True God resides, and you already know perfectly well that not one bit of this matters in the Great Big Picture Puzzle known as life on the path to freedom, or even back seat activities on the long and winding road trip to immortality.

Shocking news: You don't *need* to be over-informed, particularly if you think that education is going to come from the media or social justice warriors or the propaganda being shoved up your chute by this or that political party, or this or that guru, or this or that religious nutsack. If you really stop and examine where your political bent is coming from, you will find (100% of the time) that you have been programmed by someone or something other than Ultimate Truth, for the sad and ugly truth is that there is *no* truth in the gladiatorial arena which is the milieu of all politicians. You know this, but you do not want to believe it, because you have been so conditioned to think-you-believe in what is right and good, when you are really only a rusty mouthpiece and conduit for the bullshit that is going up your arse and coming out of your mouth in the form of regurgitated rhetoric and dangerous dogma.

Think. For. Yourself.

If you decide you really must vote, then do so. But do so 1) knowing it will make no difference whatsoever; and 2) from the mindset of silent knowing that has *nothing* to do with what you have heard or read or seen on the righteous flat screen screaming at you from the very pit of the lowest common denominator. Treat it as controlled folly[8] if you must, but it is the kind of folly that tends to have a lot of glue, making it difficult to release even when you know it *is* folly. Best not to try on that mask at all, no?

Believe it or not, if everyone voted from their heart, the world would be a beautiful paradise with trees and flowers

---

[8] Controlled folly: An immortal (and some mortals) know that everything is folly, meaningless activities enacted on a transient stage. The sorcerer-seeker may choose to engage in certain activities, *knowing* they are folly, but doing it anyway for reasons only the individual seeker could clarify.

and chirping birds and a new car in every garage and free housing and no-cost medical care for all. (And if you believe *that*, there's a bridge in Brooklyn I'd like to sell you real cheap.)

It makes no difference. Not really. I've been around long enough to see that several times over, but please don't take my word for it. Sit with your Silence. Ask your Other which way you should vote – and when he stops howling with laughter at your naiveté, maybe you will finally start to *see* that those rare few who succeed on this path do so by avoiding the trappings, clichés and false belief systems which otherwise enslave them to the consensus reality for the duration of their short lives.

Immortality isn't found in political arenas or religious agendas. If you think otherwise, you have already lost the battle.

Anyone who has been on this earth as long as I have has given up the foolish notion that bigotry, racism and misogyny will ever truly end. When I was a child (longer ago than even I can recall), I had a naive thought that by the time I became a man the insanity fueled by religious fanaticism and the delusions of politics would pass. Certainly, I thought, the world would become a better place through entropy, if nothing else. The crazy and the hateful would die out, rendering their brand of madness extinct.

Sadly, that did not happen.

Sadder still, it still hasn't.

Saddest of all, it never will.

As I prepare to go out this evening to contemplate the darkness that has nothing to do with nightfall, I hope (as I always do) that I will return at dawn to find the world a better place.

Sadly, that will not happen.

Humanity appears hell-bent on its own destruction, or at the very least, the demise of all reason, the abdication of love in favor of fear and hate.

31

Such a species cannot survive.

Perhaps it is best. Through their will and their choices, they will be their own undoing.

Relevant Comment From a Seeker

I've thought about your comment and have come to the conclusion that it applies to just about everything we tend to think is so almighty important. In reality, not much matters one wit, particularly the crap that goes to make up the consensus. When I was in my twenties, it seemed like <u>everything</u> mattered. Women's rights. Gay rights. Rah rah wave the flag for freedom, justice and the American way. But the reality turned out to be that a lot of changes came down the pipes, but in the end, not one damn thing has really changed. Sure, we have gay marriage now, but I'm sure that will come and go and come again as politics and religion continue their infernal dance, and when you really stop to think about it, most humans will live and die in a momentary flash, and all they ever were or might have been will be lost like tears in the rain.

It is virtually impossible to impart the hopelessness of politics and religion to those who still believe such things matter. It is equally as impossible to tell a flag-waving youngster that the election has already been decided, (at least 2 years ago) in some stuffy board room where assholes gather to discuss the fate and folly of their subjects (you, me and all the other "little people.") Sure, you can go to the polls and cast your vote, but when all is said and done, you are just running in place on a hamster wheel in a vast prison that might look like The Real World, but is really only a dirty little cage created and maintained by the powers that be.

If this sounds paranoid and unreasonable, I strongly suggest you take a moment to examine the lens of your perception. It's so easy (even for advanced seekers) to get caught up in the heat of whatever moment is being held out in front of us like a carrot whose sole agenda is to lure us to our death. While we're watching the cartoon characters in their political and religious posturing, time is slipping by and with every day that passes, we are that much closer to death, and that much more blinded by the things that seem to matter so much, but which have little bearing on our day to day lives. While we're focused on all those clever tricks, the brute with the scythe is posing as the magician, and laughingly herding us all the way to the grave.

When we _really_ strip away the blinders, what we See is that 99% of it is pure and unsweetened bullshit.

———

Tonight is a haiku in black ink,
tomorrow a dalliance beyond the clock.
I walk between the shadows,
immortal talisman
cast in the shape of man.

What Is Vampireland - *Really*?

In Anne Rice's books she calls the vampire world that her characters live in the "Savage Garden." I was wondering how that term applies to the night that never ends and what you refer to in <u>Teachings of the Immortals</u> as vampireland.

As I recall, Anne Rice's vampires lived in what I commonly refer to as "the world of matter and men." Even though they perceived things through "vampire eyes," they were in a somewhat organic body, even though it had been profoundly changed by their transition from human to vampire. They were like seers in the sense that many *saw* the underpinnings of the overlay (Lestat certainly *saw* this), and as a result they were one step removed from the human world.

My personal opinion is that her vampires were indeed almost completely rooted in reality. From a literary perspective, it's a splendid way to explore how humans are all trapped in that same reality - mortality, disease, death, old age, poverty - by placing the observer in a more enlightened perspective.

As to the question of vampireland, I would say that the reality of creating it is different for all who do it. To some, their vampireland will be an exact duplicate of life on Earth. They will live more or less as humans, going to work, sometimes even going through the motions of a family unit, but they do it with the knowledge that - once they are transformed, transcended or transmogrified - it's just a watercolor in the rain.

Vampireland is what you make it. Mine is often a deep dusk landscape filled with crumbling cathedrals and the ruins of civilizations that have not existed for a hundred thousand years and some. Sometimes the rivers and oceans are calm. Other times they are wild and tumultuous. It is almost always raining and so the large cats who roam the land seek shelter in the belfry of an old church where I go to plug my computer into the energetic structure of The Grid so that I might talk to others of like mind from time to time.

You can do whatever you have the power to be or do. I have supreme faith in your vision of vampireland. Make it so.

Awakening From the Matrix
From a letter to an apprentice, 2001

You have come to a point in your awakening that is perhaps the most dangerous of all. As when awakening from any sleep, there is a transition between the two worlds, where elements of each impinge upon the mind and insist on their individual but diametrically opposed realities. In the Otherworld it is true you can fly or breathe while skinny dipping under the icy waters of the river Styx, but if you tried either of these things in what you think of as the consensual reality, the results would not be pretty.

The problem is simply this: you have unassembled the underpinnings of that consensual world and used the footings to create the cornerstones of the Otherworld, but you are still in that no man's land *between* two worlds, not yet fully whole in either.

To use the analogy of *The Matrix*, Neo is "The One" insofar as he has the ability to manipulate the matrix through the projection of his Other. He will only become indestructible or immortal if he should choose to integrate the two into one. In the movie, the "program" Neo was capable of acts of sorcery, yet the body was vulnerable to being so easily unplugged. The body projects the program, but only if the body can upload the program does the body become invulnerable. Ah, so now you begin to wonder, am I hitting dangerously close to a far more personal truth?

If there is an ultimate reality of consciousness, it is simply this: consciousness is a projection of will, limited only by the

35

force of one's personal intent. I am a being of pure consciousness, manifesting at will into the being you would call Mikal. What facilitates this is the force of unbending intent. These are only words, stabbing at a concept all but alien to the human mind. You think of yourselves as organic, but are you really?

> *Are you consciousness projecting an organic body or are you an organic structure inhabited by an independent consciousness?*

The danger is that the program runs so deep that consciousness makes the program real. Because there is overwhelming evidence to support the notion that you are organic first and conscious later, you are victims of that program and it is real now whether or not it started out as real when the first human inhabited the paradigm.

The difference between us is that you are still existing within the human program, the organic matrix. To become a being of pure consciousness is the transformation we have spoken of in varying terms since our journey together began. You become pure consciousness when you pass through or beyond the state known as death. More accurately worded, when you pass *beyond* the reach or the effects of death.

This is why I tell you that you *must* make an unwavering commitment to your Intent. Without it, the will cannot manifest and the energetic force of consciousness can be dismantled by the brute's scythe, for if it has not been given a goal and a purpose into eternity, it will lack the cohesion necessary to withstand the force which could also be called Death.

Do you fully comprehend the meaning of making the commitment to your Intent? What you are fearing – this half-formed world of such terror – is what awaits you if you do *not* make that commitment, for you have truly come too far to go back to the complacency of the consensual dream.

36

You tell me. Tell me what you will become. Tell me what will happen as a result of what I will do to you. Ah, and tell me who is really going to do what to whom? Or is this a journey you are not yet ready to take? It's all right if you aren't. We can take the walk through the night slowly and enjoy the sweet scent of the jasmine blooming on the walls of Hell. It's up to you. How much of the apple do you want to nibble tonight?

This is an area of understanding that cannot be forced or even explained with any sense of sanity. It can only be glimpsed when you are ready to see it.

Before I was Mikal, I was a thought of *being* Mikal. It could be said that that thought originated within the organic matrix, but that through Intent or magic or sorcery – sorry, but the best word really *is* Intent if you stop to analyze what that word truly means – the thought-form gained sufficient energy to house consciousness. It is a paradox, yet not. It is how an organism evolves in a continuum where death is seen as inevitable.

Only when the thoughtform becomes greater than its physical matrix is immortality possible. It is more than a strong sense of identity It is also the long-term and willful application of Intent which begins to generate a new matrix capable of sustaining consciousness apart from and in addition to its original organic matrix.

I remember being a little boy in Greece and so it is my reality, yet my suspicion is that these are only memories I have given myself to explain my own existence within linear time. I tell you I am a thousand years old and some, yet I am already eternal, while at the same time an organic mortal creating its immortality – self and Other, one and the same, yet separate, yet not. This is the lost art of transmogrification, so alien to the human mind as to be labeled impossible, incomprehensible.

I am written in the blood of apples,
red and tempting to taste.
Songs of the dead
play on my fractured heart,
a rogue drummer
healing the memories
of centuries.

Within the seventh sense, there is only consciousness, but how or *if* it evolves can only be determined from within the dream, and that is *your* realm to govern, not mine.

In referring again to *The Matrix,* when the Oracle told Morpheus he would find The One, that would never have been *Realized* if Morpheus had simply sat back waiting for it to happen. It required a commitment to his own intent. And that commitment required action. What I am telling you is what I have been trying to make clear for centuries: *without an unwavering commitment to your Intent, it is all just wishes blown on dandelion fantasies.* Do you have the strength of will to *be* the paradigm you are envisioning? Do you *really*?

Self-doubts and fears are only extensions of the program, designed to trap you into voiding your commitment to intent. What is this commitment I speak of? It is simply the decision to believe what you already know. Because you *do* know it, it is not an act of faith. Ah, but unless you allow yourself to fully *believe* it, you will never act on it. If you envision it and *see* it but never really believe it, it becomes only an impotent tulpa, existing for a brief time only to fade and vanish. In acts of sorcery, believing is the only way to *seeing*, see?

To my own perceptions, I am the eternal wizard dancing over your rooftop while you lie sleeping, safe and secure in your warm bed. I am not a thoughtform alone, but I am real flesh and voodoo blood, trapped in a handsome wrapper of our mutually agreed-upon design. This is how you made me, for this is what I must be in order to do to you what I will do.

I take you by the hand and lead you into these quantum territories of the unknown because it has always been my experience that the more you understand, the easier your transition into Oz. Yes, I am pure consciousness, but that consciousness is presently and perhaps eternally assembled as immortal me, and so never doubt that my fangs are real and the blood in my veins cold as apple cider served straight from the devil's left wrist.

Ah, my loves, eat my body and drink my blood, nibble my pretty apples and sip my mushroom tea, and we'll all live happily ever after over the rainbow, beyond the horizon, in a land of jack o'lanterns and autumn leaves, yes? Forgive me, but it's close to Easter and at times I suffer from a god complex. After all, I am the only god I know, no?

I-Am the twin
escaped from the mirror.
When I find my mortal reflection
your world will end.

Gnosis: the Foresight of Hindsight

Gnosis shows you symbolic messages in dreams and activates silent dialog from the Other. How exactly do you glean information from the grid of all knowledge? For example, does the twin whisper the information or do you automatically know it? Obviously with a mortal body, there is a limit to the amount of information you can store, but an energy body is infinite I presume.

It would be impossible to explain *how* information is gleaned from the grid. Basically, it is a direct link between the self and the infinite – rather like a USB plug-in to the library of the infinite. Literally all knowledge is available, but the human mind is only capable of holding a limited amount at any given time (rather like a limited RAM). So even though the All may be available, the real secret to gnosis is being able to access that which pertains to one's specific questions – or, more accurately, the real key to gnosis is being open and available to whatever downloads come your way through your Other. Put simply – the key to gnosis is knowing how to listen and how to translate.

> *Let's say I want to use gnosis right now, to learn how to fix car brakes. How could I access the web of all knowledge and download it into my brain? Keep in mind that some people can't sit in meditation for hours to just learn something. Gnosis is a very good tool, but only if you know how to use it instantly to help you.*

Your question may reveal why most people are not able to use gnosis effectively. Think about it – if you had all the resources of the universe at your disposal, would you *really* want to waste a download on how to fix your car, when you could look up that information or take the car to a mechanic? I know the point you're trying to make, and it's valid. But gnosis generally doesn't operate that way. It's not really like *The Matrix,* wherein you download the helicopter pilot program straight into your brain. I'm not saying it's impossible – it absolutely *is* possible – but that kind of thing only tends to work for those who *have* spent hours (years, decades) in what amounts to living meditation – learning how to 1) *hear* the voice of gnosis; 2) *translate* the voice of gnosis into practical language; and 3) *manifest* the download into a practical application.

Keep in mind that gnosis doesn't work in a linear fashion anymore than time does. If an ordinary man's brakes go out, it will usually be in the middle of nowhere and at the most inconvenient time and place. If a seeker who is in tune with the infinite has brake problems, it will normally occur in front of a reputable garage or – even better – the seeker will have had the sudden insight (aka gnosis) to have his brakes checked and repaired *before* he goes out.

Gnosis is the foresight of hindsight.

The Dark Blessing of Adversity

Nothing is as it seems.

A dark blessing is something that might appear on the surface to be a setback of major proportions – either emotionally, spiritually or in the dayshine world of so-called reality. What's important is to see that some of these setbacks may be blessings in disguise; and yet, for as long as they are viewed as curses or failures, that is all they will ever be.

It must also be understood that the Other has its own agenda, and if you have given your twin carte blanche to teach you all you need to know to become immortal, that agenda is wide open and usually doesn't consist of a sunny classroom with geraniums on the windowsill and apples on the teacher's desk. More likely, the geraniums may take the form of the mushroom ally and the apple is laced with forbidden knowledge that will tear your world out from under you so as to destroy the old foundation to make way for a new one.

One of the Other's most common tricks is to play the role of skinwalker[9] in ways you cannot imagine and probably

---

[9] Skinwalker: A being who has the ability to temporarily inhabit the body of another. Any being in an immortal condition would possess the ability. In certain branches of shamanism, the shaman may invite an evolved entity (often his own double) to inhabit his body for the purpose of sharing consciousness and expanding awareness. Imagine what you might learn if you were to share consciousness with a true immortal. While certain religious groups have expressed a fear of this as a form of possession, skinwalking is normally a mutual agreement between the seeker and the entity to whom he would lend his body. Do unscrupulous skinwalkers exist? Sure. But so do unscrupulous priests.

would not believe, particularly if you are still hooked into any remnants of your dayshine thinking. Why a skinwalker? Put simply, the Other understands more than you do at this point that *love is the reason*. To that end, she will go to great lengths to get you to fall in love with her.

Sometimes this dangerous dance is confined to the dreaming and astral planes. Other times, it can sneak into your dayshine world without your knowledge or permission. You will be walking along one day, and suddenly it's as if you were hit over the head with a fairy wand imbued with love potion. *Blam!* Right in front of you is the man or woman of your dreams! It's almost the old cliché of love at first sight, and it is here that the dark dance really begins.

There's a warning in many spiritual teachings which says that the seeker who comes face to face with his Other is a dead seeker[10]. This is a truth of sorts, in the sense that if you *knew* it was your Other, if you had that certainty which can only come from advanced *seeing*, you would most likely *be* a dead seeker, for the simple reason that the irresistible compulsion to conjoin with the Other would overshadow all reason and you would find yourself surrendering to the dark desire to be consumed and subsumed by your Other – right there, just like that, no ifs ands or buts, and not so much as a by your leave.

> *This is the power of the Other – its ultimate agenda is to upload the mortal's essence and awareness so that twin and mortal become a singularity of consciousness which is forever beyond the ability of death to undo.*

---

[10]"No sorcerer knows where his Other is. A sorcerer has no notion that he is in two places at once. To be aware of that would be the equivalent of facing his double, and the sorcerer that finds himself face to face with himself is a dead sorcerer. That is the rule. That is the way power has set things up. No one knows why." (Don Juan to Carlos Castaneda)

This conjoining isn't actual death, but most mystical teachings have no real concept of what death is or isn't, and so the role of the Other is either downplayed or turned into some sinister avatar of fear which the seeker is taught to avoid.

With that said, the Other will normally only take on the role of a skinwalker with a seeker who has not yet mastered the art of *seeing* – because to one who *sees*, there is no mistaking the twin, even when it may be hiding inside the body of some other person or even some other creature altogether.

It is virtually impossible to wrap words around what I am attempting to describe here. You will either *see* it or you won't. One thing is certain: if it *does* happen to you, there will be no mistaking it and no stopping it.

When this type of event occurs – when you find yourself falling in love with this man or woman who is the Other in disguise – let it happen. Just... *let it happen*. Love is the reason, remember? But it tends to get a bit more complicated when dealing with the Other, because what you might not understand at this stage is that the twin is also the trickster – leading one to the edge of the abyss and sometimes pushing one right *over* the cliff.

Why?

Because the lover we fail to ensnare is the one that haunts us. If you had taken this dark love to its ultimate potential, the mystery would be gone, consigned to the past and done with. Unconsummated, it remains a mystery, one you might hopefully be compelled to pursue for the rest of your life.

In almost every case I have witnessed with regard to this phenomenon, the love is never physically consummated, and that is the dark nature of the dark trickster whose agenda is to hook you with the talon of seemingly unrequited love, so that you are forever chasing the muse, never catching her, always in pursuit of this perfect Other who would complete you... if only... *if only.*

Does this mean you can have no other lovers in your life? Not at all. But it does mean that you will be forever obsessed by the one that got away. In many cases, what you will also observe is that there will come a day when this perfect companion will simply vanish from your life forever. Perhaps they will move to another city. Or perhaps they will simply be different from one day to the next, looking through you as if they don't know you.

And maybe they don't.

When a skinwalker leaves its human host, the host usually has no recollection that it was ever there. Other times, the host may remember the events that have transpired, but be completely unable to put them in any sort of cohesive context. If you were to ask the human host, "What happened? I thought we were more than friends," chances are the host would give you a vacant stare and maybe even issue a restraining order. But instead of being emotionally crushed, keep in mind that this human you are now talking to is *not* your Other and never was. The human you are talking to post-skinwalker is nothing more than a befuddled host – often chosen *because* he may have a rather low awareness threshold in the first place. Harsh, but true.

What has happened in cases such as this is that your Other has given you a glimpse of what you are capable of – the *depth* of love and desire you have the ability to experience. It's what you *do* with that love that matters. Too often, the seeker may revert into a dark depression and use it as an excuse to turn from their own path, disheartened and dejected. Other times – for those who choose to *see* the dark blessing for what it is – the seeker enters into an unwritten pact with the Other. The pact reads, in part, "I, the undersigned, do hereby avow myself to you mind, body and spirit. I give you carte blanche to teach me all I need to know in order to embrace the totality of myself – even when it hurts, even if it breaks my human heart."

And it will.

And yet... the heart that cannot break also cannot love unconditionally.

And so goes the dance.

———

In response to the comments above, a seeker said:

> *Mikal, you wrote "the love is never physically consummated... and that is the dark nature of the dark trickster whose agenda is to hook you with the talon of unrequited love, so that you are forever chasing the muse."*
>
> *If I have to unite with my twin totally in order to attain the singularity of consciousness, how is it possible that this love is never consummated? Chasing someone does imply a state of not having that person, right?*

I was referring specifically to situations wherein the Other takes the form of a skinwalker.

In general, it's the *chasing* of the muse that keeps the muse always one step ahead. The Other knows where he is going, and is leading you on the journey. When you catch him (or her), the journey ends, one way or another. To be *very* specific here – either you transform/transcend/transmogrify, or you lose interest in the chase and return to the world of man and muggles.

Does this mean the love of self and Other is never consummated? No. It means the consummation is the culmination of the chase. The consummation of this union is what will change you... *forever.*

> *If you're still hooked into dayshine thinking, how is the Other powerful enough to skinwalk?*

The Other functions outside of time, so even if you have not yet fully developed her, there is a thread of possibility that

45

you *will*, and so the Other has the agenda to dream *you* into being so you will dream *her* into being. It is a paradoxical conundrum, but nonetheless valid if you really take the time to think about it.

It is the existence of all possibility that answers your question. It is through forcing that possibility to go through the motions of actually occurring that the Other is enabled to complete its agenda.

What *Is* Energy?

Energy is all that really exists. It is comprised of what we commonly think of as atoms, protons, electrons and all their various quantum cousins. When energy forms into a living thing (such as a human body) it is considered organic. When it is in its natural state, it is considered inorganic. As this begins to indicate, it is when consciousness is able to attach to an inorganic form that it has achieved a state of permanence. Energy is always in motion, always changing form.

Think around the edges of this and you will *see* the correlation between an immortal consciousness and energy itself.

Evolution of the Singularity
From a letter to an apprentice, 2002

At a molecular level, there is no difference between a radio frequency and an elephant. Both are comprised of precisely the same energy. To a mortal being, the body is an organic construct vibrating at a particular frequency. To an immortal being in physical form (transformed), the body is an organic construct vibrating at a marginally higher frequency which renders it impervious to traditional causes of organic

46

deterioration. To an eternal being (transcended or transmogrified), the body is the electromagnetic energy of the universe as an entirety. And so it could be said that I inhabit stardust and grave dust equally, you see. My body is a song you might hear on the radio, passing by your window in the night, or a sepulcher upon which you might rest when visiting old friends.

Consciousness is the receiver. The body as you traditionally think of it is a support mechanism for consciousness while consciousness goes through the process of evolving to the point where the organic body is no longer required. Sadly, most humans have lost the instinct which drives consciousness to perfect itself, and so the organism dies on the vine, obliterating any possibility of continuity. It is only if consciousness perfects itself sufficiently to exist *apart* from the organic body that it is then capable of using the universal energy to project a 'body' of your own choosing.

The perfected immortal is like a hermit crab, taking the essence of itself out of organic form to inhabit a much larger shell – the universe at large. From that quantum state, it is then possible to project and inhabit whatever manner of energetic structure (body) might be suitable. It could have the appearance of something entirely solid, but its ultimate reality is that such a 'body' would be a projection, most often for the convenience of the mortal world.

Do you hate me for intentionally leading you down the pretty garden path in the beginning, for allowing you to think of this evolution in terms of physical, organic immortality, occupying the same fragile mortal construct you presently inhabit?

If so or even if not, remember to remember: you had to learn to love yourself in physical, biological form before you could love yourself enough to project that love beyond the mortal timestream and into the infinite – the realm of eternity where I sit sipping fine red wine and the animus of autumn windsong.

Ah, but do you know that everything I have intimated to you is still within the realm of all possibility? I am still whatever you want me to be. But now the question is this: are *you* still who *you* want to be?

The most difficult part of this evolution is coming to understand the relationship between consciousness, energy and will. Because you are in mortal form, there is a tendency to separate body and mind and spirit, yet from the perspective of the building blocks of reality, all are exactly the same: *energy*. Will is the quantifiable *force* that is the product of evolution, the spark of creation that enables you to attach consciousness freely to any object in the universe, or to no object at all. I could just as easily be a man you once knew or a cold October wind. There is no difference.

> **The trick is learning to truly <u>see</u> that consciousness is the I-Am and not the object to which it is attached.**

An old friend once said that his own transmogrification became easier when he came to *see* that the body is like an egg, with consciousness being the fertile yolk inside. The shell eventually cracks to release the being within, which has evolved beyond the limits of its own environment.

Where do *you* stand at this moment in the time-space continuum? If the egg were to crack in the next instant, have you evolved sufficiently to attach consciousness simply to *itself*, or would it get trapped in the organic maelstrom of the brute and his scythe? Do you have the momentum to continue, and do you even begin to realize that it is the agenda of the consensus to stop you at all costs, because now you are a threat to the status and the quo?

There is a point within any consensual continuum when "The One" with awareness could crack the entire foundation – if not directly, then in accordance with what is commonly called the hundredth monkey effect. This is why the consensual continuum and all her phantoms fight to the

48

death, literally, to subvert the truths you now take for granted. This is why it may often seem the world is out to get you.

It is. And yet...

When the seeker *becomes* the world and the universe, she is beyond the dictates of the consensus, embedded into the fabric of the sentient universe, and therefore has become the All itself. That is the nature of immortality, the definition of an eternal being, a singularity of consciousness.

You Have To _Be_ Immortal...

Quite often, the Other will allow you to experience glimpses of the night that never ends, feelings of what it is like to inhabit the mindset of infinite eternity.

This is the voice of the muse, calling you to yourSelf.

This is the Other, showing you what it is to *be* immortal... so that you will be motivated to *become* immortal.

Autumn's foreplay:
promises written
on brittle leaves
and slate gray sky.
It teases me,
wine on the tongue
savored for a Time
before consummation.

The Dark Art of Surrender

Establishing a dialog with the Other is going to be different for everyone. For many, it is a long term process of falling in love with projections of what might be considered "creative imagination." It might look something like this:

1. Create an idea of your Other as your perfect companion – friend, brother, lover, any or all, whatever you most desire.

2. Project the image outside yourself so that it is standing in front of you.

3. Treat it *as if* it is real, which is how it is *made* real.

To some, perhaps that sounds like any kid engaging in fantasy with an invisible friend on an otherwise insignificant Saturday afternoon in the middle of summer, but guess what? That's quite probably *why* kids engage in that kind of "imaginary" world. As adults, we use words like "fantasy" or "imagination", but the reality of it in the quantum universe may be quite a different story.

As with the tulpas[11] of eastern cultures, the Other often starts out as a thoughtform. Whether it grows into an actual twin, or withers back into the shadows depends entirely on what the projector (the human self) does or doesn't do.

The key? Simple.

Surrender.

Surrender to what?

The human instinct to fall in love.

---

[11] Tulpa (Tibetan) thoughtform. A tulpa is a concept in mysticism of a being or object which is created through spiritual or mental powers. The term comes from Tibetan "emanation" or "manifestation".

It's not complicated. It's about doing what comes naturally and not backing down from it just because we become adults or because the program tells us we're being silly.

> *Remember: the program is written by the consensus, which is all about protecting its own status quo. No organized religion and no world government wants you to create and interact with your Other, because the moment you do, you no longer need them.*

Think about that.

The job security of the consensus reality depends on keeping you at your desk, in your cubicle, in front of your television, in church on Sunday, 2.5 children and a Lexus to support, 9 to 5, amen. Any doubt of this, just look around. And ask your doctor what you can do to be happier, more content with your job and your fate and all those phantoms who pose as family and friends.

Ordinary men and women live in the illusion.

Seekers and immortals live *outside* the illusion.

It's the same world.

And the Other is the walker between the worlds.

Surrender is the dark art of allowing your Other to seduce you with promises of eternal love, eternal life, and eternal freedom. And while this may sound too simple on the surface, I assure you it is no easy task, and yet once done you will discover it is the easiest thing you have ever done (once it gets beyond being the hardest thing you may ever do). Put in a more linear fashion, you must prepare your mind, body, and spirit to *allow* change – and at the same time there is a need to know what you *want*.

Most seekers fail by not having a clear goal, or, more likely, in having a goal that may be *too* specific. If you visualize change coming in the form of a check for a million dollars, you have unknowingly but very effectively screened out all other possibilities – meaning that a check in the amount of $900,000 would be impossible because your intent is set toward a single idea rather than a general (but powerful) moving *force*.

Examine your processes.

Long-term intent is a matter of visualizing your desire and then releasing the energy (a quantifiable *force*) into the fabric of the universe. When done on a regular basis, it becomes second nature – not something you think about with conscious effort, but something that flows from you like chi. It becomes an actual movement of creation rather than a simplified and static visualization. The end result is that your actions in the dayshine world begin to lead you in the direction of your intent – you begin following your vision and building it through your doings, reinforcing it through your not-doings.

Surrender to the process with joy and confidence. When you fret over it, the force of the energy itself changes and mutates and you begin to project the fretting/failure, and so *that* is what will manifest. It is only when you surrender to the power of your own intent that you will find the power to manifest it in the form of your desires.

On a mind/body/spirit paradigm, the act of surrender most often occurs in the vicinity of the solar plexus, and may be experienced as a flutter of energy that fills the chest and abdomen, radiating outward from the body in all directions. This is the force that actually travels into the extant universe to seek out and gather together the elements of your vision, bringing them together into a cohesive manifestation.

When that force can be summoned at will, the seeker might wish to visualize their intent, allowing it to project outward from the point of origin. And then, the hardest thing of all... *let it go*. Release it to the night that never ends and breathe in the quantum reality of All Possibility.

Let. It. Go.

Many seekers speak of needing to be "empty." That is simply another word for surrender. The seeker who has surrendered to his intent is emptied of stress and fear, thereby allowing room for the energetic force to manifest change, create the immortal Other, and open the door to gnosis.

That is the nature of sorcery – surrendering the dayshine self to the Other without fear, for it is the moving force of joy and what some mystics call, simply 'play', that will ignite the spark of your vision into your eternal flame.

The Other *Is*

The Other is the vessel of your immortality.

The Other is a construct of energy. (But so are you, at the core level of your existence.)

The Other can take any form or no form at all.

The Other is always what you *need* it to be, but not always what you might want (or *think* you want) it to be.

The Other is the quantum manifestation of gnosis – the teacher within – but the Other must be created before it can serve this function. This, of course, also runs into the conundrum of time being the First Fundamental Lie. There is no linear logic, so one must rely on the tools of Intent and what can only be called *magic*, keeping in mind that magic is only science not yet understood. And so the conundrum eats its own tail, back to the beginning... the Other is the quantum manifestation of gnosis.

Despite what religions and new age mumbo jumbo will try to tell you, the mortal self is the source of the Other (not the other way around). Because of the illusion of linear time, most teachings will try to tell you that the higher self descends into earthly form (a meat suit) in order to learn life lessons... blah blah blah. The reality is quite the opposite – which you will discover for yourself if you stay on the path long enough. The mortal self creates the Other as the vessel of her own immortality – the vessel of consciousness beyond the confines of the meat suit.

The Other is the self outside of time.

The Other is the self.

The Other _is_.

Unbending Intent and the Art of Gnosis

Gnosis has to find its own level. Meaning – you may be asking the wrong questions, or trying to hear answers on a frequency that isn't compatible with the question asked. The best thing is to ask your question, then send it on its way. The answer will generally come to you within a few days at most, and _always_ in the manner you least expect.

The key to working with energy is being able and willing to let it go so that it can work its magic and find its way back to you.

Think of unbending intent not as a hammer, but as a river. Unbending intent is always there, even when you might not be actively thinking about it. It is something that is part of you – ever-present, the creator of the will and the instrument of the will. It cannot be forced, but must be allowed.

Learning to let it go is a difficult lesson because one is almost always inclined to look for results, which is actually _using_ energy that is therefore unavailable for creation of your desired goal. Letting it go looks something like this:

1. Set your intent. "I want to attain a state of gnosis with my Other."

2. Project that unbending intent into the sentient, energetic universe as a conscious thought, and also as a deep-seated _desire_. This path isn't strictly intellectual or practical. It is the projection of _magic_ with the hope and intent of manifestation.

3. Release it. Let the energy go forth to find its own path (like a river).

If you continue to practice this method, the river will wind its way back to you, manifesting your unbending intent in ways that will be obvious. This generally happens right about the time you start to think it will never happen.

Growing Old on the Porch
From a letter to an apprentice, 2004

Do you feel at odds with life and time and the world at large?

If you have come to that place in the road where you and the road are truly one, where the path and she who walks the path are the same for all of eternity, then our time together on this earth is done, and this is as it must be, as it should be, as it _is,_ for if you have reached that level of accomplishment, there is nothing more I can teach you, and it is simply a matter of waiting for time to run out of time, for your mortal life to run its course, or for that moment when you will simply step out of your mortal shell and into your immortal Other. It is a time for celebration if this is the case, but I must ask you in all depths of trust and honesty… _is_ it yet that time?

There is nothing wrong with growing old on a shady porch somewhere in the hip pocket of Father Time as he walks through the woods, dusting your cabin with snow. Indeed, that would be the life I would want for you – a full and wondrous adventure – so I do not think you are understanding the level of the question. If you are at odds _sometimes_, you are at odds, _period_. This is not a criticism, but only a state of being. When you are one with the path, there is no difference between sitting in meditation or running your business or growing old on the porch.

You might find your dreams and ambitions shifting and evolving as you yourself shift and evolve. You will also discover (at a very fundamental level) that it is only through living the equation *Intent + Action = Manifestation* that any of your dreams and ambitions will ever be *Realized*. Many seekers (particularly those who fell into the trap of "the law of attraction") made the mistake of believing that belief itself is enough to achieve manifestation. It never occurred to them that *Real*izing dreams and ambitions is largely a matter of *action* combined with the underlying and underestimated force of *Intent*.

If a seeker is true to himself, he *becomes* the path rather than being *on* a path. When that occurs, every action you take is an extension of your Intent – until, eventually, what you Intend begins to manifest, even if not always in the ways you have imagined.

I'm tempted to say that you *can* have it both ways (your dreams and your evolution), but there is a long list of caveats that would have to follow, and therein lies another aspect of the darker teachings. First and foremost, what might happen if your dreams and ambitions are in conflict with your Intent regarding your evolution? Silly example #1: if you dream of going to Europe (Dream/Ambition), but you buy a ticket on a slow boat to China (Action), you are in direct conflict with yourself. Then the question becomes, *why* might this be the case? And that's where it gets darker and storm clouds begin to gather.

Examine this in your own life. Are you facilitating your journey or thwarting it? You might be surprised at what you discover.

Grasping Time

I'm having a hard time grasping the concept of the "First fundamental lie[12] of time". I know it's not linear and I know it's a sphere. But just knowing is not enough to transcend it. I must feel it and experience it, or have a further understanding with it.

Humans toil under the idea that time is a long line of events stretching from Point A to Point B, with proceedings occurring in linear fashion. The reality of it is that everything is holographic in nature. Read *The Holographic Universe* by Michael Talbot for a better understanding of this. Also, *Tertiam Organum* by Ouspensky.

Another thing to understand is this, and though I have said it many times, it bears repeating within the context of this discussion:

> ***All things exist within the realm of possibility, but only some things will be forced to go through the motions of actually occurring.***

It is the actions and Intent of the seeker which force some things to go through the motions of actually occurring, while other possibilities remain unmanifest. I mention this now, because as you become more adept at dealing with The First Fundamental Lie, you will begin to *see* that the chaos of all possibility really isn't chaos at all. Everything that happens

---

[12] The First Fundamental Lie: The human paradigm is built on the notion of Time, and so it could be observed by one *outside* of the matrix that the paradigm itself is erroneous because it has created within its subjects a viewpoint that is based on what immortals call The First Fundamental Lie. You are made of the pixels and photons of limitlessness and timelessness, yet unable to access that nature because the agenda of any consensus is to create parameters which can only limit the power and understanding of the thing itself.

does so because it is Intended by someone, somewhere, in some corner of "time."

You have undoubtedly run across my riddle: "You have to *be* immortal before you will know how to *become* immortal." That is also another way in which you can experience the true nature of "time". Put another way – you have to *be* the Other before you will know how to *become* the Other; and the only way to do this is to understand that what *appears* to be true today might not become manifest until twenty years from now. But because time is not linear, you may begin to experience the Other (through dreaming, meditation or gnosis) long before you force the Other to go through the motions of actually occurring.

How is that done?

That is what the infinite journey is all about, and it is individual to *you*. Most if not all true seekers speak of what is commonly called "the hurt" – a soul-deep longing, a sense that something or someone somewhere somewhen is somehow *missing*. The hurt is so powerful at times that it calls one out into the night to shake a fist at the stars or chase the brittle wind or converse in unknown languages with the rain.

That hurt is the energetic connection between you and your Other, and you can use it to define her/him through the art of visualization. It isn't so much about physical appearance of the Other as it is about the *type* of person you want him to be. And since the Other is a projection of the mortal self, it is about who you want *you* to be – not just on this transient Earth, but for all of eternity.

First and foremost, you most likely want him to be immortal, which is why the vampire paradigm works so well for this path. You also want him to be your teacher/guide/mentor, so it's important to give him free rein to *Go, Be, Do.* In other words, you project the Other into the infinite (beyond space and time) to gather experience which may then be communicated to you through gnosis, dreaming, meditation. The actual projection of the Other usually isn't something you do consciously. It projects itself, given the agenda stated above. It knows where to go and what to do. You don't need to tell it to go live a lifetime in Pompeii and another in France, for example. You don't need to tell it to be a starship captain or a sex slave in ancient Rome. It knows what you need to know, and it will seek its own experience, which is part of *you*, even if you don't realize it on a conscious level.

This is also the nature of so-called "past lives". They aren't past at all, but occurring in the infinite Now, through the vessel of the Other. As you progress on the path and your twin becomes stronger and more adept (yes, I know time isn't linear, but words can only define the indefinable to a certain point), you will begin to notice that you start to develop what amounts to a permanent state of gnosis with your Other. This isn't to say you will remember all of your parallel lives, nor is it at all necessary to do so. They are part of your experience base, part of the riddle, "You have to *be* immortal before you will know how to *become* immortal." If you give the Other the agenda to "Teach me and make me immortal" (just to be very simplistic), then everything the Other does in the infinite will address that command and attempt to fulfill that agenda.

The trick, of course, is that *you* in the Now are responsible for gathering your cohesion. Perhaps this will give you some dark insights into the non-linear nature of time and the role of the Other in the process of forcing *itself* to go through the motions of actually occurring.

Why is this part of the darker teachings?

Because it is when the seeker begins to truly intuit and *see* the nature of the Other and the infinite responsibility one has to him that the seeker begins to realize the infinite responsibility one has to *herself*.

There are no angels or demons to save you or condemn you. You alone hold the key to your own salvation, or your own damnation, and that key rests squarely in the infinite and eternal Other.

Undoing the Power of The First Fundamental Lie

Time is The First Fundamental Lie for the simple reason that time as it is commonly (mis)understood creates within the human being a sense that time is an entity or a phenomenon through which one is moving. In other words, the lie is the notion that time is linear (in addition to the notion that it exists at all).

Time is, at best, a quantum spherical bubble containing past, present and future – all of which are only arbitrary marks on the Lie itself, but words are sometimes necessary to describe the indescribable. Put another way, this quantum spherical bubble contains everything that ever happened or ever will – within a singularity created and inhabited by everything that ever existed or ever will. (You are *here*.)

Most humans never get as far as even considering this. Fewer still ever reach what follows, but which is crucial to any seeker looking for the door to transmogrification.

Put simply, this quantum spherical bubble contains, in addition to everything that has or will be forced to go through the motions of actually occurring, the infinite *possibilities* of what might best be described as "the roads not taken." Or, if you prefer, the infinite possibilities of everything that has *not yet* been forced to go through the motions of actually occurring. Parallel realities, no less real than the one in which you currently exist.

There... do you feel it? That little ache inside your head that happens when you encounter a truth that is bigger than yourself, yet is a secret you have kept from yourself all along? Often it is uncomfortable, for it threatens the status quo of existing programs and beliefs.

What does it mean?

Within the quantum spherical bubble of time exists the infinite possibility which is the assemblage point of the Other. Once you have that thought, it becomes possible to *see* that the door to transmogrification lies within one of two (or an infinite number of) possibilities.

1. The process of inhabiting the Other (the totality of yourself) must be forced to go through the motions of actually occurring within the "timeframe" of your linearly-perceived mortal life – in other words, by doing The Great Work. Or:

2. Because both time and mortality are illusions within the broad spectrum of infinite energy, you also have the option of opening your eyes inside the assemblage point of the Other so as to inhabit the totality of yourself through the manifestation of a spontaneous parthenogenesis which would essentially shift your awareness from the organic mortal form into the immortal and inorganic energy body which exists within the quantum spherical bubble containing all possibility.

The seeker who can *see* this wholly holds the power to manifest their immortality, because that, too, is a point of perception within the realm of all possibility. From that perspective, you are already immortal.

And yet...

None of that will absolve you of the need to manifest the back story of your immortality through whatever actions you take which force that state of being to actually *occur*.

The First Fundamental Lie is at the root of all the other lies – or you can call them programs or belief systems. The First Fundamental Lie can actually be simplified to read: "All things die." Or "All things are mortal."

As long as a seeker believes *that* (or any variation of it), The First Fundamental Lie has ensnared him. Even if the seeker might undo *all* of the other programs, as long as The First Fundamental Lie remains in effect, transmogrification is not possible.

Why Vampire?

Why is the term vampire applied to the Other in
Teachings of the Immortals? Is it primarily a question of
aesthetics? In what way is the practice or teaching vampiric?

The word is intended to alert the seeker that she can be
anything she chooses to be, provided she is willing and able to
do the work of transformation[13], transcendence[14] or
transmogrification[15]. The myth is as ancient as humanity
itself, and as mysterious. Additionally, the teachings come
directly from silent knowing, where a vampire is recognized
to be a transcended immortal (originally human), and rather
than try to hide the word for the sake of those who might be
frightened or offended (the consensual reality's most common
reactions), it seemed reasonable to present it as it was
presented to me when I was a very young seeker, and keeping
in mind that it was my predilection to be drawn toward the
mysterious and the mystical rather than the mundane.

---

[13] Transformation: essentially a form of so-called "physical immortality" whereby
the seeker transforms his nature from mortal to immortal. This is the most limited
form of immortality, because if a comet smashes the earth, one's immortality goes
to pieces. While it might be considered "immortal" by some, it is really only a
form of extreme longevity, as opposed to transcendence and transmogrification,
either of which result in a being of pure energy.

[14] Transcendence: wherein the seeker sheds his body through the process known
as Death. Those who transcend become pure energy, existing at a level of
consciousness/awareness without any physical form whatsoever. They may inhabit
and project the form of the Other, or remain ubiquitous.

[15] Transmogrification: an Intentional transference of all life energy (consciousness,
awareness, individuated memory) from its mortal human coil into its immortal
energy body. Because the energy body is a quantum state, it may take any form the
seeker Intends, and may change form at will, depending on the skill and
experience of the transmogrified individual. Transmogrification is generally a
long-term process, often requiring years of intent, meditation, and perfecting of
abilities.

It should be pointed out that the parallels between the vampire mythos and the quest for immortality are plentiful, as you will hopefully *see* as you read this volume.

What makes it vampiric? The seeker does. One could achieve the immortal condition and carry on like a stock broker, but that generally isn't the case for those who would be intuitively drawn to these teachings. The nature of a vampire is to take energy (lifeforce, aka animus) directly from The Source. For some, it might mean taking energy from other human beings, though that is generally the practice of those who have not yet learned to take animus from the universe at large. To others, it might involve taking energy from blood from a donor, but this dangerous practice results from too much exposure to Hollywood movies and horror novels. It can certainly be done as a form of personal sexual preference, but hopefully precautions would be in place – and *hopefully* those doing so would understand that *the drinking of blood has nothing to do with attaining the immortal condition.*

If you were to observe an immortal taking energy from a human, it could be assumed (wrongly) that he was taking blood from the human's neck (or anywhere else). What the vampire is really doing is taking the animus. This can be done *without* any exchange of blood and without harm to the donor, and it is generally an intimate and often sexual ritual. Put simply – it is a *lifestyle* choice rather than a biological need.

Keep in mind that the universe is made entirely of energy – it is abundant even in the most isolated corner of the void itself. As a result, there is simply no reason to take it from other lifeforms.

> *Real immortals have transcended human form and do not partake of organic matter (including blood). A transcended or transmogrified being is an inorganic being who may project a seemingly organic form, but the essence of such an individual is that they are (ironically) beings of light, or – more precisely – beings of <u>energy</u>.*

The Darker Teachings are meant both literally and spiritually. Everything begins with a thought – including the thought that immortality is a viable possibility. Of course, there is more to the myth than humans have been led to believe. Vampires are very real – simply another type of lifeform – and so the key is knowing the difference between what Hollywood has injected into pop culture and the reality of the thing itself.

The word vampire is a description of one type of eternal being. All transmogrified beings are eternal beings, but not all eternal beings are vampires.

You can be anything you choose to be. The only limitations are those you impose on yourself.

As social culture and trends have changed – just in the short time since *Teachings of the Immortals* was published – even the language has evolved somewhat. You may note that what I used to refer to as a vampire I now most often refer to as, simply, an immortal. What I previously referred to almost exclusively as the "twin" or the "double" is now generally known as the Other. The reasons for this are plentiful, but ultimately it's a matter of clarity. While the word "twin" or "double" is accurate, it has the potential to conjure images of an exact copy of the mortal self - a doppelganger. The Other knows no such limitations, and while it *can* be a replica of the mortal self, it can also be altogether different, gender opposite, young or old, or even altogether alien to one's humanform perceptions.

Think outside the box. Words are only descriptions. *See* beyond the ordinary when seeking the extraordinary.

> *Immortality is hidden*
> *in old books not written*
> *until next week,*
> *and violins strung*
> *with the sinews of madmen.*

The Agony of Immortality

In <u>Teachings of the Immortals,</u> you discuss the immortal's pain – "the solitary pain that makes coyote trickster sing." Is this the same as that ache that you've mentioned that guides the seeker into looking for what she seeks?

They are somewhat different but also closely related. The ache/hurt/want/need that drives seekers is most often felt at times when there is an open window of opportunity – when the seeker is at a crossroads. The test is whether or not the seeker will *embrace* that ache, or if they will, instead, run back to the safety net of existing comfort zones.

Many who claim to be seekers really aren't. They are more along the lines of armchair philosophers. A true seeker will embrace the ache even if it eventually kills him, for a true seeker realizes that comfort zones are really only inescapable sand traps on the driving range of Hell. But by embracing the ache, the seeker also surrenders to the realm of all possibility, knowing in advance that not all roads lead where one wants to go, and some roads can collapse under one's feet and plunge one into the hungry abyss.

As a result of all of this, the seeker becomes what is commonly called a warrior – though I don't particularly care for the taste of that word, since it implies a conflict or battle with the world at large. In the bigger thumbnail, seekers aren't really at war with the world or the environment or even with themselves. If there is a war at all, it is a war between Chaos and the Knowledge which dwells behind the silence – but this is something most don't realize until they have tilted at numerous windmills along the way.

The dark truth is that true seekers usually end up losing everything an ordinary human being would consider to be of value. The seeker eventually discovers that she really doesn't have a niche in the world of matter and men – because an even darker truth is that the world of matter and men is a society comprised of the lowest common denominator of human beings, and the cost of membership is your soul.

I have heard certain spiritual teachers telling their adoring acolytes that, "Yes, young Timmy, you *can* have it both ways! You can be President of the United States *and* achieve immortality – and you can do it in five days or less if you buy into this expensive seminar I'm sponsoring!" The reality is a bit different, and since I have no reason to need people to like me, I also have no reason to tell them pretty lies.

The dark truth is that most seekers (there are rare exceptions) find it virtually impossible to be a card-carrying member of the consensus reality while simultaneously being committed to the journey.

OMG, did Mikal just say seekers are destined to fail in the real world? The bastard!

No, that's not what I said, but there is some truth to it nonetheless. I mentioned rare exceptions, yes? Yes. They do exist – those who have become successful in the world of matter and men, and who also manage to succeed in their ongoing spiritual evolution. What makes such an exception? Hard to say, but it probably depends largely on their predilections. Those rare exceptions might simply be more hard-wired to be stalkers as opposed to dreamers (to borrow terminology from Carlos Castaneda). Put another way, this path might be more *natural* to a stalker than to a dreamer. Then again, it might not.

Most who choose the path of the immortals are dreamers – creators, artists, writers and the like. *If* these people (dreamers) can find success in the world of matter and men, they may become one of those rare exceptions, but it is indeed rare, and it is certainly an exception. Most dreamers seldom find that niche of sustainable success, and so they are conflicted – torn between their commitment to themselves

66

(their art, the path, etc.) and the need to survive in a world that places no value on creativity.

Those who maintain their commitment to the path may find themselves at odds with the world in general. The struggle for survival in the short term (the material world) goes to war against the struggle for survival in the long term (the path, immortality). The resulting spiral is a force to be reckoned with, and one that often drags the seeker down into a maelstrom of despair.

Solution, you ask?

There is no easy solution other than to quit. Grab your belongings, hold them tight to your chest, and run straight back to the safety of the mundane world. Of course, it will be a finite journey and you may not be able to let go of those nagging things you've learned along the way. Even if you are safe in the arms of mommy and daddy and your molesting uncle, you will always know what you have given up.

I am not going to tell you this journey is easy or simple, or even possible at times. This is why it is said that you cannot choose this path. *The path must choose you.* Only if it does will you be able to overcome the downward spiral that is created by the spin-and-drain cycle of the consensus. If you are lucky, perhaps you will emerge from the maelstrom to find your niche and become one of those rare exceptions. I want you to believe you can.

As for the "solitary pain that makes the trickster sing," I would say that this type of pain is more akin to the state of being that many immortals experience.

The solitary pain of an immortal is the pain that results when you look at those you might dare to love, and realize they are finite beings who will live and die in a very limited segment of the hologram. And while it is possible for immortals to step backward or forward or sideways in the hologram of time to visit old friends, it is always confined to the lifespan of that individual, and as such is immune to a Creator's instinct to take what is mortal and make it immortal

– not for any altruistic reason but for the Creator's own self, for the alleviation of some measure of loneliness, for the preservation of some lotus petal of love.

And so comes the realization that the hologram is infinite, but also finite, and yet it also appears to be indelibly inked into the icy fabric of The First Fundamental Lie.

This, again, is only the tip of the iceberg's tip.

> *I walk among dark ruins*
> *remembering a lover's teardrop*
> *on a headstone*
> *long away gone.*

The pain that makes the trickster sing might best be understood in the speech Roy Batty makes near the end of the classic film, *Blade Runner*.

> *"I've seen things you people wouldn't believe. Attack ships on fire off the shoulder of Orion. I watched C-beams glitter in the dark near the Tannhäuser Gate. All those moments will be lost in time, like tears in rain. Time to die."*

Even the immortals know nothing is truly forever because forever itself is a loop on the belt of The First Fundamental Lie, which will, in time, cease to exist until the next loop begins to set it all spinning again.

The immortals will still be there, of course, and so will the pain that makes the trickster sing.

Addendum

I cannot really say if the "solitary pain" becomes more acute after transmogrification, but it does alter. It often shifts from hope (in the mortal manifestation) to despair (in the immortal manifestation). Simply put, the mortal *hopes* for salvation or meaning or simply for peace; the immortal fully *knows* there is no salvation other than what can be found through the Self, the only meaning that exists is that which one creates, and the only peace is the finality of the grave. (Now do you see why these are the darker teachings?)

Most people – including most seekers – want-to-believe that achieving the immortal condition brings answers, serenity and renewed hope. The truth, however, is a bit different. While I would say that many of the immortals I've known are content, few are happy in any definition of the word I've encountered.

OMG, is Mikal saying immortality is a depressing and eternal dose of despair?

No, not at all. I'm simply pointing out that becoming immortal doesn't answer all your mortal questions nor give you lasting peace. What it *does* give you is a lot more "time" in which to pursue them, or create the answers, meaning and peace within yourself.

> *Will the immortal continue to remain unfulfilled in some way?*

I would have to say yes, though with certain qualifications. I do not consider myself unfulfilled, but I *would* consider myself a restless being, never at peace and always searching for whatever lies beyond what is presently known. If it were otherwise, I might easily become complacent (the flaming arrow of the true death).

It is the unknown that draws us forward, keeping the bow string of awareness taut and always at the ready. Becoming immortal doesn't automatically increase one's intelligence or hand one the keys to the kingdom of all knowledge. It is still necessary to hone awareness and intent, moving always toward the *next* evolution.

The immortals realize that nothing is *truly* eternal except eternity itself. Suns will flame out or softly fizzle. Galaxies will collide and collapse. Time will fold in on itself like a cheap taco. And nowhere in all of that mumbling and rumbling is there any sense of meaning. Even the immortals are struggling to evolve *beyond* the cycle of universal birth and death, beyond the big bang or the big collapse or whatever physicists are saying today to explain the things that happened trillions of yesterdays ago.

The immortals, more than most, know that science is only another religion, and what is "true" today is proven "false" tomorrow, and so it all goes, on and on in the spiral that circles the drain which lies at the center of all creation.

Nothing is real.

Yet everything is real.

And so even the immortals are plagued and cursed and blessed by the solitary pain that makes the trickster sing. Without it, there is no reason to take even one more step. And that is the moment when even the immortals die – if not into the True Death, then certainly into the oblivion of spirit.

> *You also mention that the vampire is "at constant war with death" and relives it endlessly. Is this the cause of the pain? I think I understand the war, but perhaps you could elaborate. I was under the impression that once immortal, one had essentially conquered death, so how is it that the relives death endlessly if he or she is beyond death's power to undo? Is it literal like the re-death/turning experienced in* Sons of Neverland[16]*, or is it more an eternal experience of the myriad lives/deaths (which we mistake for reincarnation) that the Other has gone through during the process of becoming immortal?*

Once one has transmogrified or transcended Death, one cannot actually die in the manner humans die. Once transcension or transmogrification occurs, one is an individuated consciousness in energy form. How that form

---

[16] **Sons of Neverland:.** A vampire novel by Della Van Hise.

70

appears is irrelevant at that point – whether seemingly physical or just a free-floating vaporous apparition. In *Sons of Neverland*, Della explores the possibility that vampires who were turned in the traditional fashion may dream and re-dream their transformation night after night. If the transformation was pleasant, the dream may be wildly erotic. If not, the dream is a nightmare. I find that approach an interesting parallel to the actuality of it.

The transmogrified/transcended immortal is constantly renewing – and I mean this literally. It is like an energy field that is self-perpetuating, an individuated entity moving in and out of the universal web of energy at will. In *Sons of Neverland* the vampires renew their energy in this manner, literally re-creating themselves every night in their dreaming. It is the same for immortals. We recreate ourselves by moving in and out of the universal web of energy, and so we are beyond the ability of death to undo.

> *Does the immortal experience emotional pain at viewing all the bright sparks that allow themselves to be taken in by the deceiver program, telling them they will eventually die? Does the vampire somehow experience those deaths as his own, even though he cannot die?*

While immortals certainly *can* experience the death of something else as if it were their own, most choose not to, for obvious reasons. Occasionally, if one is sufficiently bored, even an immortal may choose to enter into a death trance with someone they have known, or even some*thing* they never knew at all (such as a wild animal). The reason to do so is to make an attempt to *see* beyond the threshold of Death, through the eyes of the dying one.

To my knowledge (and here is another dark dose of the darkness) no immortal has ever seen anything on the other side of that so-called "rainbow bridge."

> *Whether man or beast, prince or pauper, microbe or marsupial, the only thing ever <u>seen</u> is the silent darkness of the No-thing. This does not mean there is nothing. It only means that even an immortal's enhanced perception cannot <u>see</u> beyond that fatal veil.*

That's the way of it, round and round we go again and again, worlds without meaning, life without end. The saddest immortals I've ever known are those who sit by the eternal flame at the edge of the abyss, looking out beyond the last galaxy's end and saying, "This is all there is." It is those who sit by that same flame on that same cliff and say, "What lies *beyond* even this?" who truly have the stamina for immortality. All others need not apply.

The need to believe in *something* comes from the awareness of mortality. That awareness is perhaps the most terrible curse and the most profound blessing humans have ever received. It is only when that foundation of false hope crumbles that the seeker really has the opportunity and the vital necessity to create and nurture one's own "great beyond." Failure to do so results in the recycling of all you have been or known. Tears in the rain...

Run-run-running In Place

> *I'm always rushing to get things done but they just reappear in some other form, a constant influx of distractions and make-work that is never really finished.*
>
> *Yesterday for example, I was trying to upload some stuff to eBay. Just did it about a week ago but in the interim everything had changed, so that meant clicking around to figure out the new procedures, which meant watching This or That tutorial and reading This or That holy help reference, and by the time I'd made all the necessary changes, 4 <u>hours</u> had passed and it was only a $10 item So even if I sold it*

right away, that would mean I might make about $1.75/hour
when you factor in all the fees, not to mention the psychiatric
visit that's pending because of all the typical internet bullshit
that's making me feel like a puppet being jerked around on
the strings of the consensual reality.

You must be doing something right because it is the nasty habit of the consensus to throw obstacles in the path of anyone who has begun to *see* the world for what it is. In so many ways, technology may be the thing that ultimately destroys the human race, or at least kills the human spirit.

Since I come from a time long before the internet existed, I can say that it is a behemoth when it comes to the wasting of time and energy. While it has its advantages, it is a fact that humans are attracted to it like moths to a porch light, circling and circling until, eventually, they fall on the doorstep, just empty vessels with tattered wings. And sadly it has become almost a necessity if one wishes to survive in the world of matter and men.

What to do?

You've taken a positive step forward simply by *seeing* it for what it is. But the darker truth is that it isn't something you can fix. In so many ways, technology was the downfall of Atlantis (another dark story for another dark day) and it will be the downfall of the current civilization. That is simply a fact.

The only way to stop run-run-running in place is to simply *s-t-o-p*. Every moment is but a click on the clock of The First Fundamental Lie, and as such is altogether insignificant *unless* the seeker hones the awareness that the only way to stop time is to stop marching to its ever-increasing tempo. If there are things you really *need* to do, do them first. If that becomes impossible because of the hoops you are being required to jump through to get from A to C to B and back again, ask yourself if the task itself is even remotely necessary at all. Remember the old adage... "A difference that makes no difference *is* no difference.

Now what to do as you stand face to face with an army of Agent Smiths?

Never forget – Agent Smith doesn't *really* exist, at least not in the manner most believe.

> *Agent Smith is little more than a mouthpiece of the consensus, whether he takes the form of a scolding parent or a pompous evangelist or a certifiably mad politician. As in martial arts, the goal is to deflect his blows rather than attempting to battle him head on.*

If it is his voice you hear in the background, telling you to "Hurry up and get this work done so you can move on to more and more work," you need to quietly and gently question his authority. He has none, you realize. His only power is what you give him. If he is telling you to run-run-run, ask him where it is he wants you to go? You'll quickly discover that he is only an impotent toadie, a reflection of a distorted world.

I've read the thread on the Immortal Spirit forum called "Dayshine's Fury, but Why?" many times, and one thing that jumps out at me is a comment you made which reads:

"Vampireland is wherever and whatever you create it to be. Whether it is a kingdom of One or thousands is entirely up to you. For example, my kingdom has a sign on the gate that says, **'Entry by invitation only.'** I do not invite many, and some overstay their welcome very quickly."

What I'd like to know is how to get to that point, where you can disappear behind that gate and leave the crazy world spinning in its own shit. I'm not there yet and I'm afraid I may never get there if I can't get some sort of control over my environment.

The only way to *get* to vampireland is to *be* there. The only way to kill an immortal is to make him believe he is mortal. You have to *be* immortal before you will know how to *become* immortal.

Maintaining some degree of sanity is often a matter of realizing that you may be the one sane man in a world full of madmen. You are out of step with their agreements, as has been the way of seekers since the dawn of that nasty lie known as time.

What you are experiencing illustrates perfectly why seekers need to be creating their own kingdom at all times. Vampireland exists in the heart, and you may call it whatever you like. Heaven. Valhalla. The Other Side. It is built with the sound of leaves hurrying down an October road, the scent of night snow in a forest of evergreens, the ruins of ancient Greece, cemeteries where every grave is empty. It is a place you may return to in dreams, gnosis, or meditations, and one night, you may find yourself able to step into it in what might be called a "physical" form.

Vampireland is something you take with you, an edifice you inhabit at high noon or deepest midnight. Am I saying it isn't real? Not at all. Everything begins with a thought and is built with Intent.

When you *become* the path – embracing it and embraced *by* it – you will no longer be running in place, because every step you take is one more step in the direction of your dreams.

Signs or Synchronicities?

Seems like the universe is throwing a lot of anvils in my path and at my head. I can't figure out if these are signs or just weird synchronicities. A couple of examples. My business has been iffy for awhile, and this past year it just keeps getting worse. Every time I get a handle on it, along comes something else.

So my question is this: what do you think when all sorts of shit starts hitting the fan all at once? Is this some sort of message from the Other that I need to make a change, or is it just random bullshit brought on by living in a world full of assholes and knuckle-draggers?

The syndrome you are describing is not uncommon among seekers, though it might have a wide range of possible causes.

It could well be that your Other is participating in what seems like your downfall. From what you have described, it could also be that your business endeavors have consumed far too much of your energy and if you are not seeing a commensurate return (income vs. outgo on an energetic level) chances are you are caught in the leg trap of the dayshine world without necessarily realizing it on a conscious level, and so your Other takes it upon herself to create those "signs".

But even if the Other is showing you where and why change is required in your dayshine affairs, she may not show you *how* to go about manifesting those changes.

I once worked closely with a seeker (let's call her Ana) who owned a major corporation, successful and profitable. Without explanation, things took a grim turn and before too long things went from good to bad to downright ugly. When she asked me to examine the situation, I immediately *saw* a vision of her Other pulling the kinds of strings that would result in the collapse of the organization altogether. Why? Because even though Ana was one of the most intent-driven seekers I've ever known, she had gotten trapped in the role of feeding and maintaining the corporation at the expense of feeding and maintaining her Other.

A hungry twin is a dangerous twin and will stop at nothing to point the seeker back in the direction of her own evolution – *even if that means the destruction of the seeker's dayshine life.*

When the Other is created with the intent to teach and assist the seeker in achieving the immortal condition, it isn't limited by the traditional rules of common courtesy. It is a ruthless and relentless *force* that doesn't stop until the goal is achieved or until the mortal self succumbs to the dust and the dark and distant whistle of the ghost train[17].

With that said, it becomes crucial to examine the things in your life that seem to be going wrong. Sometimes it is just attrition resulting from Life On Planet Earth. Other times, it will become obvious that the Other is meddling in your affairs in an attempt to save you from yourself. Literally.

The other side of this rather cursed coin is that Agent Smith is alive and well and living in your head unless you have taken the steps to eradicate him entirely (and even so, he often finds ways to resurrect himself from the ashes of one's self-doubt and the maelstrom of dayshine chaos).

Agent Smith is the force in direct opposition to your Other – and for that reason alone it is vitally important to distinguish between the actions of Smith and those of your twin. If it is Smith meddling in your affairs, you will have to

---

[17] Ghost Train: After the mortal has created his twin, should he fail to achieve transmogrification, there is a theory that the fully-developed twin has the ability to step back in time to a point when the mortal self was still in the mother's womb. By entering the mortal self *prior* to birth, the twin is then born into the same body as the mortal self the agenda being to enforce the mortal self's evolution by existing as the internal teacher. For anyone with an understanding of quantum mechanics, this is not so far-fetched, since time is not linear but actually a sphere, where all events are non-local. Put simply, the 'ghost train' runs back and forth on the same track until such time as the mortal self and immortal twin conjoin to create the singularity/totality of both.

confront him and hopefully defeat him. If it is your Other, I suggest immediate surrender and a course of drastic change.

Know the difference first. Then take action.

God, Gods and the Light

I am brought back again to the question that plagues me day and night – how and why did this human existence begin?

I have always liked this explanation:

> First shaman created the world, and when she realized she was lonely, tore out half her heart and put it into her dreaming body so she would never be alone. But because the double was made of Spirit, it left her all too soon and went to dwell in eternity, where its siren cries call her back into the Infinite. This is why the heart has two chambers and why the shaman walks the earth with one eye on the world and the other focused on that which has no name.
> –Quantum Shaman: Diary of a Nagual Woman

While it is impossible to know where the first humans originated, I'm inclined to think it is largely a matter of random evolution. Though that answer might not be emotionally satisfying, it is the most likely when held up against the idea of a creator-god. I do view the universe as having awareness – if not direct personal sentience then certainly an awareness of its existence which must have begun as a matter of spontaneous parthenogenesis[18].

---

[18]Spontaneous parthenogenesis: something coming into existence out of the nothing, with no evident cause. It is theorized by the author that the universe

Having explored the ins and outs of consciousness, and having found myself in "the land of the sentient dead" a time or two, it is my belief that consciousness can and does spontaneously spring into being when the No-thing is sufficiently oppressive.

If consciousness did arise from the nothing, if some particular accumulation of atoms came together in such a way as to create a *thing* in the *No*-thing, there would perhaps come a time in the No-time when that *thing* would scrape together enough rudimentary awareness to rise up out of the darkness and proclaim, vehemently, *"I-Am!"* In fact, there is a Biblical parable about precisely that, though the misperception which follows is that this entity was therefore God simply because it was the first.

Therein lies the danger of erroneous conclusions.

Assuming my theory is correct – something from nothing – it is also likely that this entity was able to guide others toward a similar awakening – much like Morpheus in *The Matrix*. But Morpheus wasn't God and it's important to remember that God doesn't exist simply because you *want* him to. Man has a tendency to think of anything he doesn't understand as gods or demons – entities in league with his plight, or in opposition to it – the age-old conflict between good and evil, light and dark.

When the seeker begins to realize that those states are only humanform assignations, it becomes possible to finally *see* that each individual is their own god, their own devil, and their own Other. If you want to make Biblical comparisons, the Other is the rib torn from the self to create an Other *like* oneself, but also more far-reaching. The problem is that even the most advanced seekers may have certain belief systems so deeply ingrained that even they are unaware of them, and

---

created itself from the void through an act of spontaneous parthenogenesis - a thought that willed itself into existence by saying *I-Am*. It could be visualized that the act of transmogrification is closely related to an act of spontaneous parthenogenesis – a willful self-creation beyond the existing paradigm.

when confronted with the truth about gods, devils and twins, this darker Knowledge may actually break their blasphemy bone and cause them to run screaming into the night. Denial is a dangerous perch in the storm of enlightenment.

Even advanced seekers who believe they have reasoned it out come face to face with their own demons when attempting to truly and absolutely and finally justify within themselves that we were not created by a loving god or cursed into slavery by spiteful demons.

SPONTANEOUS PARTHENOGENESIS

Before anything we currently think of as being part of the universe existed, there was only an immense void, a nothingness, the abyss, a black hole which had gathered into itself all matter and energy. Yet from the nothing, literally a thought which created itself in an act of spontaneous parthenogenesis, the universe sprang into being. A thought creating itself because it needed to exist as an entity separate from the void. It required <u>identity</u>. It demanded <u>life</u>, yet the only way to achieve life was to create itself from the nothing and hurl itself out in all directions, a sudden sentience breaking apart from whatever had contained it previously. Because it was a creation of will, it created itself with perfection, which is to say it gave itself all possibilities and, even more so, it gave its component parts, including us, the ability to evolve in order to adapt to changing circumstances within its own continuum.

If we think of the void as containing all of matter/energy, then the universe is the stage of time, and both together create the continuum of space/time and matter/energy.

*In its creation, it gave all the beings who would eventually exist within itself the ability to continue through evolution, for the ironic thing about the creation of the universe is that it gave all it had. **It won't interfere in the affairs of man because it <u>can't</u>.** There is nothing left of "it" except all these individual components that comprise the* *all, so there is no intelligence sitting outside the universe who can intervene in its destiny. In its creation, it used all its "parts" to create the whole, which means it used its full intelligence, its whole awareness, its absolute will, and in doing so, it automatically created each atom of itself with those qualities. For that reason, each of us, whether man, animal, stone, vegetable, air or distant sun, possesses the blueprint for our own unique evolution. In creating itself to survive, the universe gave us the ability to evolve...*

It seems inconceivable that the universe came from anything but a thought, an incredible force of will breaking free of whatever held it together before its spontaneous parthenogenesis. Because we are part of that creation, springing from the same quantum source, we also possess that same strength of will within ourselves, the will to survive, to be more than mere fate has sanctioned us to be by virtue of existing within the known universe.

Just as the known universe must have existed within whatever continuum previously held it, so do we exist within it, but just as the universe had to break free of the void in order to achieve its own separate continuity, so must we break free of the known universe if we intend to evolve beyond it.

-Quantum Shaman

The Darkest Truth

Perhaps the darkest dark truth about 'reality' is that what most ordinary people accept as real and right is altogether unreal and wrong, and so it stands to reason that more than a few seekers along the way have been offered a cup of hemlock for their morning tea, or shuffled off to the gallows for the crime of insurrection or blasphemy or a dozen other hollow words, all of which come down to only one thing: a threat to the status quo which must be squelched lest it take hold in the

81

hearts and minds of otherwise docile sheep suckling at the teat of society and ultimately becoming just one more mutton chop on the table of the dayshine king.

The truth is that most seekers feel compelled to share the truth about the truth, and reveal the lies about all those social "truths" which Man has been happily accepting since long before Socrates rocked the boat and Plato revealed the nature of the cave. Others come to mind, of course – whether scientists seeking quantifiable truths or seekers exploring what lies beyond the moment of enlightenment. Galileo. Magellan. Buddha. Jesus. Mohammed. Joan of Arc.

Whether executed and persecuted, or eventually just chopped out of the story by the brute with the scythe of "natural causes," the pattern here is too bleak to ignore, and if you think it will be any different for you, think again. Even if your name is never heralded by another living soul, what you have undoubtedly already discovered is that your circle of friends is already shrinking, and the warm familial embraces that once greeted you have turned instead to cold stares or fake smiles worthy of a zombie's lips just before he announces that he would very much like to eat your slippery brains.

Some of you have said you want to go back – but now you've come too far because the dark reality is that you can't unlearn what you have already learned. You may attempt to ignore it and hope it will, like a fatal tumor, go away when the sun comes up – but in that same deep vein, you've also discovered that you are already within the night that never ends, and so any possibility of sunrise vanished entirely when your Other stripped away the blinders and you opened your eyes inside a moment of enlightenment, and in doing so, *became* the sun, moon and stars at the heart of your own universe.

And so the sun has already risen and forever set and it is *you*. Yet try as you might there is simply no way to enlighten the mortal mutton chops all around you, and so the light within you shines on a world it often seems only you can see.

That world is the door to the Otherworld which exists far beyond the dayshine realm, yet simultaneously penetrates it and overshadows it in the same way a magnificent storm may cause it to appear that there is no sun and no blue sky, yet all are individual components of the same world, each one part and parcel of the other, mirrors facing mirrors to create and then reflect an infinitude of choices, each one based on the application of Intent and the willful manifestation of Will.

Knowing this gives you no special super powers, of course. But knowing it *might* occasionally bring some peace or comfort when those around you look at you as if you are a stranger, or find reasons to be elsewhere on that Friday night when you've always-since-youth gone to the pub together or laughed at the latest bad movie just to have a reason to share one another's company.

Knowing there is only One World (divided infinitely by perception) may sometimes give you the ability to *see* that your friends and family and co-workers aren't aliens or evil tyrants. They are simply lost souls sucked into a society that thrives on their obedience and docility just as you yourself once tried to be a good little boy or girl. But eventually you discovered that the call of the wild was really the call of the sane, and you gave up the social norm in exchange for... *what*?

There are no promises or guarantees on this path, no certainty that you will make it home. This is precisely why many (most) eventually abandon this path altogether and try to go through the motions of a normal life – spouses and babies and picnics in the park on a sunny Sunday summer afternoon. And yet, there is always an ache deep in the heart of those who turn back, a Knowing that the sacrifice might have been too high, yet the Knowledge that the path, once abandoned, may never reveal itself again.

What to do?

There is never an easy choice. Sometimes the pain of loneliness and despair becomes too much and the lures of the dayshine world are too tempting to ignore. Other times, the seeker comes to *see* that the only choice is learning to love the ache/hurt/want/need that drove them out into the night in the first place. She might learn to even cultivate the loneliness and welcome the melancholy as new friends – guides and mentors along the road to immortality.

One thing is certain: this road is twisted and fraught with dangers and inevitable losses. It will not make you any friends. It won't make anyone love you. It might get you killed. And yet... for many it is the only road possible.

> *Why does the path _not_ give you friends, make people _not_ love you, and possibly kill you? Is this just the default? I've seen firsthand the immense power I can have over phantoms, and clearly you yourself have this sort of influence. So what is it that makes a seeker such a threat?*

Once a seeker embarks on this path and attains a certain level of awareness (let's call it a minor degree of enlightenment), the result is that she no longer *sees* the world in the same way those who might be considered phantoms see that same world. The seeker begins to realize that she is a stranger in a strange land, and – worse – the phantoms possess enough rudimentary awareness to recognize that she is a threat to their comfort zones.

How?

In the sense that the seeker now *sees* that there is an alternative to phantomhood – and *might* begin to expect more of them than they are willing to give. Not that the seeker has any power or ability to change them, but the phantoms do not wish to be reminded of their own folly, but instead choose to go on existing in their world of lowest common denominator thinking, doing the least amount of work possible (spiritually speaking), and resisting any change that would result in the destruction of their world as they know it.

The threat to them is not minor. It is catastrophic!

As the seeker progresses on the path and attains a deeper degree of enlightenment, she might choose to abandon the world of matter and man entirely (thereby diminishing her threat to the status quo). Or she might choose to challenge the consensus in subtle or not-so-subtle ways. It is when these challenges are issued (whether through the written word or direct one-on-one contact) that the "enlightened one" has become a direct threat to the phantoms' world.

This is why Jesus and Joan of Arc and other prophets met a nasty end – not because they were wrong, but because they were *right*. The fact that their words were later warped into religiosity is neither here nor there. If you were to examine what they were actually *saying* (as opposed to how it has been distorted by their followers) you would discover that they are saying the same thing I am saying or any other true *seer* is saying. They are offering humans a "way out" that involves keeping one's identity, transcending the consensual matrix, and transcending even the threshold of Death. But the problem is that the phantoms, and particularly The Powers That Be (and I include The Church at the top of the list) insist that there *must* be a middleman – someone who is the savior, and an organization to intercede between the lowly humans and the almighty god(s).

And therein lies the problem. All humans (even those who may be considered genetically stupid or even genetically damaged) have within themselves the ability to *be* a Jesus or a Buddha or a Mohammed *without* any intervention by any organization, without any savior to pluck their souls from the eternal torment-du-jour (pick the hell or purgatory of your choice here).

So what's the problem, you ask? Simply this: you have to *be* immortal before you will know how to *become* immortal. In *this* case, meaning – you have to *do* the work required to strip away the programs *before* you can be sufficiently free of the programs to claim your birthright as an immortal spirit.

Nobody wants to do the work. It's not easy. It *can* be fun, but most people don't see that. And so they will fight for their false belief systems that tell them they are already immortal, they already have an eternal soul, and all of the other bogus beliefs that have held the consensus together for centuries. And if *you* get in the way of those false beliefs, there's always a nasty end waiting for *you*, too.

In the immortal words of Monty Python – "Out the door, line on the left, one cross each."

Melancholy

Melancholy is the name of the human daughter I never had.

She lies in the grave of the wind on those deepest nights when the candle has burned out and you are left with your own thoughts in a silent world that has no end and you think everything has been a trick of the mind and love is not real but only a clever companion created from desperation and despair. She sleeps in the catacombs of the abyss where doubt that anything can survive or evolve nestles in her eye sockets and forms dust nests in the darkest corners.

Melancholy rises zombie-like and tries to haunt me whenever I look at those I have turned, and they turn with terrified eyes away from me, breaking my heart forever and forever. Melancholy is wary, and comes when least expected in the mirror, in a song, in the scent of a chimney fire at dusk, at the sight of a falling star. She thinks she's poetic but mostly she's just a nuisance, a wannabe muse that has attacked so many immortals throughout time.

I ask myself, why the ugliness in this world? I believe it comes from human despair, which goes along with being human, and for which I know no cure, not even this path.

Faith, Belief and *Seeing*

How does one eliminate faith and still believe in order to See?

Belief isn't required in order to *see*.

It's important to understand that faith and belief are often used interchangeably, but that is clearly not wise. Faith implies a blind belief and adherence to some sort of doctrine – something you read in a book, something said to you by a teacher, something pounded into you by social standards.

A lot of people have "faith in God," but no one has ever seen God. If you ask those people *why* they believe in God, they will give you all sorts of mumbo jumbo answers, few having anything to do with logic or even with magic. "The Bible says so," is often the most common response. "My daddy believed in God and his daddy before him," is another common groaner. Faith requires no thought, no responsibility. It just requires blind, sheep-like adherence to dogma.

Belief is *usually* based on at least some *minimal* experience. "I believe the sun will rise tomorrow because it always has." Granted, it may not, but we have *reason* to believe the sun will rise, whereas we have *no* reason to believe in God. One makes sense on some level; the other is a fairy tale so often repeated it has become a living dogma.

Seeing has very little to do with faith *or* belief. *Seeing* is what happens when one emerges beyond the programming and simply *sees* the world as it is – which includes perceiving energy directly. When you really *see,* you are beyond any need for faith or belief. *Seeing* is direct interaction with Knowledge.

Seeing is Knowing.

Is Your Mind Really Your Own?
A brief history of "the foreign installation"

Programs aren't always just belief systems. Programs can and do become self-sufficient, self-evolving and – worse – self-protecting. I tend to harp on *The Matrix*, but that film did a brilliant job of illustrating how these programs grow, evolve and adapt to protect the status quo.

Have you ever been having a harmless philosophical discussion with someone close to you, and suddenly it's as if they become possessed by the voice of Cthulu? One minute you're talking about the potential advantages of organic eggs, and the next thing you know, Aunt Matilda has grown 6-inch fangs and launched into a venomous diatribe about how the hippies of the sixties upset the apple cart and unleashed the hounds of Hell onto an otherwise peaceful Beaver Cleaver world; and if you don't believe in God, you're going to go to hell, young lady; and if you think for a moment that *you* can slip the noose of society, politics and death, think again, because you're nothing more than a handful of dust breathed into life by the sweet baby Jesus, and you should be down on your knees thanking all the angels and Republicans for that roof over your head and that food in your belly; and you'd damn well better vote in that next election because every vote counts and every opinion should be heard, but keep your mouth shut and speak only when spoken to, because that's what a good young lady *does*; and never mind that everything I'm saying is a contradiction because *that* is how the program works. Amen.

It spews mindless rhetoric until one either walks away from The Machine altogether, or succumbs to the program out of sheer mind-numbing self-preservation.

I've been asked what the purpose of the program actually *is*. What I have observed over a long period of time is that its *only* purpose is to preserve the comfort zones and create submissive zombies who serve The Machine. Anything that might potentially rock the boat is attacked vehemently.

In the Toltec practices, this is known as the foreign installation (aka "the flyer mind"). Some say the foreign installation is an alien intelligence that farms humans for its food. A common belief is that the individual components of the foreign installation (known as the flyers) survive by draining humans of their energy, and the only way to continue their feeding is to remain unseen and unknown. Clearly, the best way to do that is to keep the population docile by creating a consensus that maintains obedience through the *belief* that one is doing "the right thing."

Humans think their minds are their own, but are they *really*?

My personal take is that the foreign installation is nothing more than a habitual series of patterns – created not by aliens but by the human tendency to be followers instead of leaders or even rogues. In the big picture, it may not matter. Whether the foreign installation is an alien or a hive mind created by the lowest common denominator of human thinking, the *only* way to break out of it is to *see* it for what it is. And the best way to do that is by unraveling the programs, one by one, until eventually they all crumble at once when one truly *sees* the world as it is (which is another definition of *seeing* energy directly – observing the underpinnings of the program that create the program itself).

Once you *see* the programs and begin to shed them, the foreign installation becomes keenly aware of your insurrection and begins to throw Agent Smith at you in the form of beloved Aunt Matilda and just about anything and every*one* else. The warrior's battle, therefore, is not only with the foreign installation, but with the Self – because it will *always* be easier to toe the line, be a good soldier, and get with the program.

Freedom comes at a high price.

Not all who embark on this path will see it through. As I've said in the promo for *Teachings of the Immortals* – only one in every 10,000 who read the book will achieve the immortal condition.

Are you The One?

Change and Not-Doing
From a letter to an apprentice – January, 2004

It's unfortunate that as civilizations become increasingly complex, more rather than less is required of each individual in order to survive. It is one thing to hunt and gather. It is another thing altogether to be *forced* to hunt and gather to subsidize intangibles such as insurance, taxes, rent, wi-fi and the like. When civilizations reach that height is when they fall, because when the souls of the philosophers wither and die, the society loses its spirit and its collapse is inevitable. When one lives in the constant *pursuit* of happiness, happiness itself is naught but a carrot chased by an exhausted horse.

The slaves of today's world are machines – computers and cell phones and other minions with technological DNA. Ah, but the problem is this – the slaves have become the masters and the philosophers have turned to dust and the world is slowly dying from the inside out.

What to do? For starters, you simply *must* devote time to the silence. Not only meditation and gnosis, but also not-doing[19]. It is only in the silence that you can hear your Other speak. If you want to change, start there. For one hour every day, choose a not-doing in the silence. Take a walk. Or sit on the porch and observe the not-doings of hummingbirds and mischievous squirrels. Within a few days, you will begin to

---

[19] Not-Doing: Activities which allow the mind to do other things while the body is otherwise engaged. Example: washing dishes while gazing out the window. Picking wildflowers. Counting stars. Petting a puppy.

realize where the chaos in your day-to-day life is coming from, and then you will have a better *seeing* into how to heal it.

Write in your journal, even if you think you have nothing to say. You may be surprised to learn that your Other speaks best through pen and parchment, words of gnosis harvested from the night. That is a Doing,[20] which is also necessary, and best done shortly after your not-doing. The two are directly connected what you realize in the not-doing becomes intrinsic to the Doing. If you are even moderately disciplined in this, and practice the not-doing for a week, you will see the pathways to change which will *become* the change itself.

Death is always stalking you. That is not my Doing, not even yours. It is just what is. Grief has the power to destroy you, because grief is love undone to your human perceptions. You have seen too much of death, and the energy pulling you toward the other side is a dark gravity which must be released. The ghosts are pulling you into the grave with them for that is their nature, just as it is the nature of the immortals to exert an equal pull in the opposite direction, thereby maintaining equilibrium.

You need internal change. To wish for external change can be inspirational, but it can also become detrimental if it is an all-encompassing fantasy without any action behind it. The dream devours you without manifesting. The sorcerer's trick is to define what is desired and bring it into manifestation through a relentless Intent. If that is not what you intend to do, if your evolution is only an idle dream, then it becomes like a tulpa feeding on its master. That is why it is crucial to wholly recognize your desires, and to state them with clarity within the process of creation. *Do you know what you want?* Most don't.

In the context of your visions of what you want out of life, it is also crucial to know the difference between what is a fantasy and what you Intend to manifest into reality. How real

---

[20] Doing: an action done with conscious awareness to focus the mind.

is your cabin in the woods? Is it what you only *desire* or what you truly *Intend*? And if it is what you Intend, how will you manifest it within the realm of all possibility?

Intent creates its own pathways, but that is where the dark danger lies. You don't have the luxury of waiting for Fate or Providence or guardian angels to show you the way, so the question again becomes – what will you *do*?

If you evolve sufficiently and take the longer road through the darker woods, you may grow old on a vine-covered porch in a cabin in the woods by the sea, and we will meet at the moment of your transcension somewhere on the bridge between this world and the next. If you *don't* change, there is every possibility you may lose your way and run the risk of losing yourself forever.

One thing is certain: it is in your unity with your Other that you will find your greatest strength. If you are at odds, you have already lost.

Love is the reason.

The Super-Position of the Assemblage Point

The super position of the assemblage point is nothing. And it is everything. It is nowhere. Yet it is everywhere. It does not exist within linear time. Yet it is the entirety of time as well as the absence of time.

If you were to visualize the All as a marble which might be held in the palm of your hand, that would give you an idea of the super-position of the assemblage point. The marble contains everything – all of space and time, all of the past and the future, all things that have happened, and (most importantly) all of the infinite possibilities which have *not* yet been forced to go through the motions of actually occurring. From the super-position of the assemblage point – which might be described as non-local and ubiquitous – the entirety of the All is accessible as possibility, and yet only the doing (localizing) will result in direct personal experience.

It is from the super-position of the assemblage point that the Other functions. When I have said that I am the fire in the canyon or the intangible sparkle of light captured in a raindrop, those statements are not metaphor or poetry, but an actuality of experience. From the super-position of the assemblage point, all things exist as the potential for energy. It could not even be said that what is as yet unmanifested is energy. It is, instead, the *potential* for energy, which is made to manifest by intent and an application of Will.

> **It is through the intent of the mortal self that the will of the Other may be invoked.**

When you ask how this may impact a seeker in the now, consider that it is the mortal self who dreams the Other. As I have said countless times: "*You* are the creator of reality. I am only its servant."

It is when the mortal self summons intent (an active *force* of energetic creation) that it could be said, "The self is dreaming the double." To follow that thinking further, it is when the Other localizes his energy and manifests experience through the application of Will, that it may be said, "The double is now dreaming *you*."

The mortal self operates from a fixed position of the assemblage point (fixed, meaning from within a human lifetime), whereas the Other is summoned from the super-position of the assemblage point – which can manifest or localize anywhere within or *outside* of the space-time continuum.

I have lived a thousand lifetimes and died a thousand deaths, and yet I am Whole and eternal because there is the awareness of free Will – and my Will is to remain *I-Am* regardless of where or when that *I-Am* manifests in the material world – a seamless, unbroken awareness existing throughout space-time and beyond.

What most humans fail to recognize is that they themselves are the source. *You* are the creators of reality. Even if the double is Dreaming you, it is because you (and *only* you) have chosen through actions to Dream the double. If there is an oversoul or a super-position of the assemblage point, it is not because angels placed it there like stars in the heavens, but because you yourself placed it there through the energetic force of self-awareness.

If you were to ask the question: "Which came first, the self or the Other?" the answer is simple to one who *sees*. The self is the source, though many would tell you otherwise, because it is easier to believe in some already-immortal overmind than it is to take upon yourself the heavy responsibility for *creating* that force as a singularity of consciousness.

Put another way: the gods exist, but only if the one true god creates them. There is only one true god, and that is the one for which humans have been searching for centuries, but always manage to overlook when gazing at the reflection over the bathroom sink. And for as long as one searches externally for what is internal, one will find ways to convince oneself that one is an impotent sloth, when in reality, each one of you contains the full and complete power of the entire universe in a single thought.

Having awareness of this enables the seeker in the now to more effectively direct the power of her own intent, which in turn Dreams a more cohesive Other.

Intent is the architect. Will is the power to manifest the architect's Dreaming.

Dreaming Real

Never forget that Dreaming refers to all forms of thought-manifestation – dreaming while asleep, dreaming-awake, visualization, meditation, and so on.

As you progress on your path, you'll discover that your Other becomes stronger and will begin to take on a life of his own.

> *As you become more Whole, you will begin to see the Other for who and what it is – the projection and manifestation of your evolution, the vessel of your awareness beyond mortal life.*

Space and time are entirely irrelevant to the Other. The Other is the self in eternity, and because it is not limited by the confines of space-time, it exists in the past even though it might not be created until the future, and it exists in the future even though it may have lived a thousand lifetimes in the past.

All are part of your evolution.

The Other will stop at nothing to facilitate your growth. Once you have given him the command to lead you through your transformation/enlightenment/transmogrification (whatever term works for you), it's like giving carte blanche to a supreme ninja master. Your Other can project itself onto anyone or anything at any time – which may give some deeper insights into another of my little riddles:

> *Look for me*
> *in chimney smoke and stardust,*
> *in the cry of the coyote*
> *or the Sanskrit of the lightning.*

There are no limits to what the Other can do.

Land of the Living Dead

Music is entirely subjective. We like what we like for reasons we might never understand. My main concern with music and all forms of entertainment is that it needs to be approached with awareness in order to avoid the subtle (or not so subtle) programming messages that are inherent in the thing itself. My primary exposure to rap music, just to pick on that genre for a moment, has been a genre that glorifies and promotes violence, racism, misogyny, and a general negativity that does nothing to redeem itself.

Keep in mind that I'm not an expert. I don't listen to rap or hip-hop largely because I don't like the feeling that I'm being assaulted – both with the music and what amounts to a shouting out of someone's radical opinions. Put simply: it's a *sound* thing.

I have no problem with someone being dark or negative *if* it is a platform from which they can emerge and evolve. But when it becomes a glorification of negativity (whether in music, film, art or other medium) then it is a programming mechanism which teaches its followers that these feelings are okay, normal, and to be encouraged. As a result, perhaps it's no coincidence that a lot of today's young people have such an utterly fatalistic, nihilist, loathing attitude toward life itself. Nothing has value – not even Life. It's why things like 9/11, Columbine, Sandy Hook, Boston, Orlando and Las Vegas can happen – the people who are perpetrating these horrors have no respect for the simple breath of *Life*, and the pain of that drives them to do things they would not do if they held different belief systems (even *false* belief systems, for starters). Better the shooters should believe in a god that doesn't exist, fearing his wrath or craving his love (equal motivators), than to live in an empty hole where one's soul is supposed to be.

People do terrible things when their lives are devoid of all meaning. They have no sense of Self, no purpose for being on the planet, so they have no reason not to strike out at the rest of the world. This is why I so *very* strongly caution seekers – if you're going to remove all your programming until you are zen-empty, it is vitally important to have a new and hopefully more stable foundation on which to stand.

The problem with many of the lost souls who perpetrate this type of violence is that they have either 1) stripped away all sense of purpose in their life, usually as a result of social/peer pressure or even bullying, but *without* replacing it with any alternative belief system, or; 2) they have literally been programmed to violence by the world in which we live.

Did you know most broadcast television is filled with embedding – what used to be called subliminal advertising? Back in the olden days it consisted of a manufacturer inserting a single frame into a movie reel. You're sitting there watching a movie and suddenly you crave a Coke. No coincidence. You were just *told* to crave a Coke by a single frame of film spliced into the movie that says, "Coke quenches your thirst! Go to the lobby and buy a Coke right now!" And like a good little robot, you go to the lobby to buy a Coke. The eye doesn't see the single frame at all – it's moving too quickly – but the brain sees it and reacts accordingly.

Nowadays, the embedding is much more sinister. Awhile back (maybe 10 years ago) there was a lot of info on the internet about this, but most of it has been cleaned up. (Read: it has been shut down). What it amounts to is that anyone with enough money or power can subliminally embed all those television shows that people sit in front of, night after night, year after year, decade after decade.

You think your mind is your own? Guess again. Unless you are *keenly* aware and scrupulous in your day to day practices, you are not an individual, but an extension of what someone else wants you to be. Your government wants you to be a complacent consumer, for example, believing whole-heartedly that the 9/11 tragedy was an act of foreign terrorism as opposed to the domestic terrorism it can clearly be *seen* to be by anyone who has the ability to *see*. The pharmaceutical companies want you to "ask your doctor" about their products, and therefore it can be further determined that they want you to be sick so you will be a good customer for years to come (until they finally kill you and the next generation takes your place).

It's endless and it's insidious – and of course most of you probably don't believe it because you have been programmed *not* to believe it. There's a label for it: it's just another "conspiracy theory."

Or is it?

Try a little experiment if you don't believe me. Turn off the idiot box and leave it off for at least a month. First, you'll find that you don't really *need* it – it's just a tool of distraction. Second, if you *do* turn it on again (and if you're smart, you won't), you'll *maybe* start to *see* just what an intrusion it is – that big ugly eye sitting there in your living room.

What you also might not know is that *it* might be looking back at you and listening to everything you say. No, that is *not* a conspiracy theory. It is very real technology engineered allegedly by Verizon, and for which Verizon applied for a patent in 2012. The fact that they were only then applying for the patent obviously doesn't mean they have been good little girls and boys. If the technology exists (which it does), you can rest assured *it is already in use.* So, unless you're an exhibitionist, I wouldn't advise any sexual escapades in front of the tv, even if it is turned off.

I'm not making this stuff up. Do your own research. It's part of waking up, part of changing not only the way you *think*, but the way you *live* – which is really the *only* thing that will get you even close to the possibility of transmogrification. As long as you are programmed by the world at large, *that* is the foundation on which you are standing. What you think or believe is irrelevant for as long as you are hooked into and controlled by something other than your own Will.

In *Teachings of the Immortals,*, I expressed it to an apprentice like this:

> Consider this from the corner of your third eye: when I said I would destroy your world I meant it literally, but the truth is that I'm slipping you the tools with which to cut the bars of the prison yourself. Ah, but the darker secret is this: *the prison is a living entity as much as a cage and because it is such an interwoven part of you, the cutting away of the consensual disease must be performed simultaneously with the transplantation of superior replacements lest the cure destroy the patient altogether, yes?*

Why am I harping on this? *Because it is the cornerstone of the darker teachings.* If you think for a single moment that you are immune to the programming of this matrix in which you live, you are already lost.

> *The only way to kill an immortal is to make him believe he is mortal.*

The world really *is* out to get you – because that is the program that runs the world. Whatever it is that is programming you *is* trying to kill you – because *that* is how the dayshine world maintains its status quo. It isn't even really a matter of the world having a death wish. It's just that it's easier to "get with the program" than to stand against it. It's easier to be a mindless zombie than to build the new foundation which is the cornerstone of your individuation.

Don't take my word for it. *Please.* Do your own research. That, too, is part of the process of building the new foundation.

Undoing God

How do I dismantle my belief in God?

You dismantle your belief in God the same way you would dismantle any other belief. Look at *what* you believe, ask yourself *why* you believe it, ask yourself *when* you began to believe it. What you will discover (I guarantee this!) is that you believe in God because you were *told* to believe in God, and for no other reason. God was offered to you as an explanation and a comfort zone, probably by parents, but it is no more real than the Easter bunny. Just another fairy tale, but one that has become popular for the same reason as Christmas: follow the $$$.

> *There's a guy who says he can help me with my gang-stalking situation – he told me it's caused by demons and if I'm Christian it would stop.*

Excuse me for being brutal here, but your guy is an idiot and may get you killed. You can rest assured that your gang-stalking situation has nothing to do with demons, and being a Christian won't protect you anymore than throwing salt over your shoulder and shouting "Patronus!" at the top of your lungs would protect you. People are assholes – no demons required. What you believe won't protect you from them – only what you *do*.

> *I believe in God because I think he's protecting me and, I'm not willing to give up that protection.*

If God were *really* protecting you, you wouldn't be stalked by gangs. Think about it. You just said it yourself: "I *believe* in God because I *think* he's protecting me."

What you believe and what you think are irrelevant in the big bad world. The only protection you have is within yourself and what you *do* with what you Know.

———

When the commentary above was posted on the Immortal Spirit forum, I received a private message from this seeker, telling me this isn't the path for him, and we are parting ways. Put simply – he quit. This is, unfortunately, a very typical reaction when one finds oneself between the comfort zone of existing beliefs and the potential obliteration of those beliefs. I will say that I had been somewhat gentle with this seeker from the start, but it was (and remains) my Intent to offer honest guidance and insights to those who seek my counsel, even when that guidance might not be popular or tenderized. In plain English: if you want to achieve the immortal condition, you won't get there if I handle you with kid gloves and a silver spoon in your mouth.

The path to immortality is both enlightening and simultaneously brutal, for it means confronting those foundational programs that hold your world intact, convincing you that you are an individual when the reality is that – until you are unplugged – you are nothing more than a hollow feeding tube within the matrix.

One of the most difficult programs to dismantle is the belief in God - any god or deity, but let's just tackle this from the perspective of the Christian God for the moment. The bottom line is that most people who believe in God do so because they were *programmed* to believe in God, either directly or indirectly. In the Western world, Christianity is the dominant religion and so it is heavily embedded in society, culture, even in the media; and despite the yada that there is a separation of church and state, the Christian religion has also infiltrated governments, schools and even the work place.

Most children are exposed to these ideas from an extremely early age, whether intentionally or unintentionally, so it stands to reason they grow up with some idea that the sky tyrant is not only watching over them, but counting their sins on some cosmic abacus, while simultaneously keeping track of good deeds to know who's been naughty or nice. Oh – sorry – that's Santa Claus - I tend to get them confused, because at the end of the day there is really very little difference between one fiction and another.

Sorry to rattle any cages or trample any fragile tendrils of faith, but for as long as a seeker clings to a belief in God, she is disempowering herself completely just by virtue of the implications of the God-program itself. For as long as the seeker places god outside of herself, she is giving away her power to an entity no more real than the tooth fairy. In fact, the tooth fairy may be *more* real, for the simple reason that one's parents take on the role of hiding eggs or exchanging quarters for teeth, whereas "god" remains an elusive and evasive fairy tale whose sole purpose appears to be punishment and reward according to the dictates of a book written *by* men *for* men, thousands of years ago; and in all that time, no one has seen God as anything other than a misshapen frog-like being on *South Park..*

For your own sake and your own potential evolution, you need to understand: God is a crutch. Most people are, unfortunately, too programmed by the church to ever see through the indoctrination which has made them mindless sheeple. Most people would cower in fear or burn me at the stake for even daring to suggest that their god is nothing more than a malignant hoax perpetrated on Man *by* Man for reasons having nothing to do with salvation or evolution or any other grand and noble cause. God is the cash cow of the church. Nothing more, nothing less.

If God exists at all, *you* are God, for *you* alone are the creative force in charge of your own destiny. You have unlimited power. You have immortality at your fingertips.

102

And yet, whether you realize it consciously or not yet, you have been conditioned by your society and culture to see yourself as just a grain of sand on the bottom of a vast ocean, a powerless slug at the mercy of The Fates, an impotent "wretch" who can only be saved by Amazing Grace.

Even if you don't actively believe in God (or any other deity), you are not free of "god" until you have come face to face with my personal mantra, first communicated to an apprentice over two decades ago. *"The destruction of faith is the beginning of evolution."* Ask yourself what you believe, why you believe it, and if it is really necessary to get you through your day. Maybe it is. Probably it isn't.

In the commentary above, the seeker's decision to quit is, unfortunately, the most common response when someone bangs their head against the sudden realization that what they believe and what they know are two very different things. The seeker believes that he *knows* God exists, when the reality is that one cannot know what one has not personally experienced. Millions of people *want* to believe and so they *choose* to believe, and will fight to the death to maintain the status quo of those irrational, illogical, impossible beliefs.

God doesn't want you to live forever. If he did, he wouldn't have placed you in Harm's way. He wouldn't have made you mortal.

Predator, Prey or Bystander?

> *I can appreciate hunting as a sport of recreation, but not wanton, unnecessary slaughter. I eat what I kill. What's your stand on that?*

Because humans are largely self-indulgent zombies, they cannot be trusted to do anything within the reasonable limits. I say "limits" because the species that doesn't recognize its limits eventually dooms itself to extinction – which is what the humans are facing, and a fact that grows more dire every day. Of course, that's if we believe the planet is dying and the earth is about to be hit by a comet come Thanksgiving Day, 2025.

When the white man came to the new world, he hunted the buffalo to near extinction, blasting away for sport, which was, as you say, wanton slaughter. But that's the problem with sport. It recognizes no reasonable limits despite laws and common sense to the contrary, and so it becomes disrespectful to Life itself. For a single moment of a human's pleasure, an animal is asked to give up its whole and unfinished life? Imagine if the grizzly bears and the mountain lions decided to hunt humans for sport. It's purely a personal opinion, but I see no reason whatsoever that man should need or want to hunt for sport. It flies in the face of what mystics refer to as "the right way to live." To take a life solely for one's own pleasure is clearly *not* the right way to live.

> *To use the vampire paradigm, a vampire that does not revel in the hunt – the absolute rush of knowing that hunger will soon be sated for a time, the vampire that doesn't kill and feed – isn't a vampire to me.*

Be careful not to get caught up in the words and the descriptions. The vampire paradigm is a powerful one when one is seeking immortality through the Other, but there is a danger (evident in your comments) of getting lost in the Hollywood assignations at the expense of the reality that underlies it all. Never forget that true vampires feed on *animus* – not on blood, not on humans or animals, but on the energetic flow of the universe at large. One does not need to hunt it, because it is all around us all the time. It is in the air, in the stardust and the moonbeams and the intangible reflections glittering on the sea.

The vampire who has evolved through transformation, transcension or transmogrification doesn't revel in "the hunt" because he recognizes that even the hunger is not real, except

104

as an extension of one's physical or metaphysical form. The juicy steak Cypher longed to return to in *The Matrix* was no different than the porridge of the real world. That being the case, it is illusory to think that one is more real or satisfying than the other. In the big picture, we all live on one single thing: animus.

Yes, it is a savage garden. As I have come to see it, the hunt always turns inward. What you cannot find within, you cannot find without. What we are really hunting is the next breath, the next sunrise or sunset, the next thing to love or despise, the thing that gives meaning to the vast and terrible abyss in which we find ourselves.

That is the hunger as I have come to see it: we hunger for the light, knowing it will reveal the encroaching darkness.

Eventually, if we are very lucky and very diligent, we come to *see* that we are the darkness. And we are the light.

As the old Hopi prophecy goes: We are the ones we've been waiting for.

The Stamina for Immortality

In the 1994 film, *Interview With the Vampire,* there is a line of dialog spoken by Armand: "So few have the stamina for immortality."[21]

Many may be drawn to this path, but few will ever complete it – not because they lack the ability, but because they lack the stamina – which might also be defined as the long-term intent not only to *allow* the impossible, but to *do* the impossible.

Just words, of course. What most will hear is, "Mikal said blah blah blah and I think he's full of shit." Such is the crumbling tower of Babel, which is another interesting analogy and allegorical tale as it pertains to the long and

---

[21] Interview With the Vampire; Anne Rice

arduous journey to vampireland. But perhaps *I-Am...* full of shit, that is. Who's to say?

What you must ask yourself is if you have not only the stamina for *being* immortal, but the fortitude for *becoming* immortal. One of the most frequently asked questions I hear is, "How long is this going to take?"

Forever.

Because it is... for *ever*. Thus the riddle takes on a new meaning: You have to *be* immortal before you can know how to *become* immortal.

If you are asking that question and feeling perpetually impatient, you may need to ask the *next* question, which is simply, "Do **I** have the stamina for immortality?"

Dying is easy. Living forever is hard. Sure this is what you want?

———

So how long *is* this going to take?

It takes as long as it takes. Some seekers may achieve the immortal condition in five years. Others may take fifty years. Others never achieve it at all.

It's not the destination that matters as much as the manner of traveling. Put another way – you can get to Poughkeepsie a lot faster by plane, but you would miss out on the world's biggest ball of twine if you didn't go by car. Of course, if you went by car, you would miss out on the oldest tree in the forest because you weren't hiking. And so it becomes a matter of *experiences* along the way that go toward building your identity, your awareness of self and Other. There are no shortcuts.

Nothing wrong with some goals, as long as they are in perspective with regard to your core agenda. If you want to be a rock star, for example, part of your *journey* would be learning to play the guitar and sing on key (well, not that all rock stars sing on key, but that's a whole other kettle of cheese worms).

Your identity is comprised of your experiences. If you're racing to the finish line (which doesn't even exist), you are missing out on the very things that define who you are.

Emptying the Hour Glass of Time
From a letter to an apprentice, 2003

Immortals are not prisoners of time because each moment is its own eternity in the Now. You may see that as only prattle, but I assure you it is the key to gaining some minor semblance of control over the demon of time.

> *When you are unfocused, time fragments and runs faster, because when you are doing 10 things at once, you are using 10 times the amount of time and energy, yes?*

Think about it.

When you are fragmented, each fragment has its own life and its own agenda, its own internal dialogue. On the other hand, that which is immortal and eternal experiences each moment as an eternity, unbroken, and so life is an endless and unbroken series of events, memories and manifestations, a single golden filament of consciousness existing both inside and outside of time, but always originating in the Now. That which is fragmented lives sometimes as many as 5 lifetimes concurrently, each overlapping the other and each requiring its own measure of time and energy, so the end result is that time *seems* to compress because more of it is being used, as if 5 people are drinking from the glass instead of only The One.

What you have to do is to inhabit the *I-Am* at all times, and do it with conscious awareness. This may sound easy or trite, but it is the work of a lifetime, and it is the key to your own cohesion. Too often, I fear you are inhabiting the fragments rather than integrating their energy into the *I-Am*.

The Destruction of Your World

I know something horrible is soon to happen, but I can't put a finger on it. I'm trying to deal with the concept that all I ever believed is basically a lie, and the things I used to depend on aren't really there, and now this feeling of impending doom.

You are being hit with the same syndrome most seekers face at some point, which is best described as "the destruction of your world." At a certain point on the journey, one begins to realize that nothing is what you have been taught to believe; the humans with whom one shares the planet are largely phantoms; all previously comforting belief systems are naught but fairy tales; and the mortal self is dust in the wind.

It can be overwhelming, but it is also a blessing in disguise, for it is the motivation and the inspiration that will drive you to *do* the impossible because there is simply no other choice. It is often this devastating mental/emotional state that causes the seeker to realize that the *only* thing standing between himself and the abyss is the power of Intent. You have no choice but to climb out of the illusions and the dayshine delusions, because now your eyes are open, and you realize no one and nothing can do it for you. Yes, it is sometimes debilitating, but the balance in that equation is the impetus it provides.

It's much like standing in an open field two miles from a force 5 tornado. It turns your way – that gripping, sickening horror of what you see in combination with the awareness that all you know is about to change forever.

Have you ever been in a situation where you logically and reasonably *should* have died... but didn't? Let's use your tornado example. By all rights, the tornado *should* obliterate you in a flash, but instead you realize that you are still alive and the tornado turned at the last minute. You have to ask yourself: *Why* did the tornado turn? Did it turn because of wind velocity and vector, or did it turn because God turned it, or did it turn because *you* willed it?

Be honest with yourself when you think about situations such as this. While it is possible that it turned because of wind velocity and vector, and while it is *not* possible that God turned it (because there is no extant god I have ever encountered), it is far more likely that the force of your own Will turned it because *only* by willing the impossible would you have the ability to keep living, and *that* is the prime directive of every living thing: the next breath.

> *Part of allowing the impossible is the fine art of getting out of your own way lest you step in your own droppings.*

Put in less crude terminology, when you Will something – truly *Will* it as opposed to idle wishing – it is a quantifiable force that knows no limitations. In Biblical terms, it is stated that "Faith the size of a mustard seed can move mountains." You know me well enough to know I am no believer in faith, but if we substitute the word "Will," the equation takes on a whole new meaning. The actual movement of Will occurs at the level of energy.

Will is the mind of spirit,
the heart of energy,
the manifestation of magic.
I-Am Will, therefore I-Am.
Let there be light,
and darkness to hold it.
Let there be Life.

Will is a force beyond all words, beyond science's attempt to explain it. *That* is why the tornado turns.

Directing the Will

In the past we've talked about trying to summon the will, and you seemed to be apprehensive of the idea. I understand that the will is more of an overarching, higher will that spans your entire self across your entire timeline, and could perhaps be considered a facet of the real you, as opposed to the idea of focusing it from inside time in an "I'm going to concentrate really hard right now and try to will this t-shirt to change from red to orange" sense. How does a seeker direct his Will?

The true will is a living force. It cannot be summoned by direct command, but only through circumstance. No one can predict what that circumstance may be, or if it will occur even once during an entire lifetime.

The Will is generally directed by the Other, though it is possible that the Other may choose to manifest the Will through the vessel of the mortal self. I say this because when you use words like "direct" this falls under the heading of attempting to control the uncontrollable force. Intent is also a force, but as a comparison, if Intent is a nuclear bomb, Will is the big bang.

Can the Will even be summoned on an individual level, or is it simply determined by the totality of your choices and experiences and then left to act on its own?

It is usually the product of long term Intent, though there are exceptions. It can manifest instantaneously if circumstances demand it. A woman lifts the hypothetical bus off of her infant – not because she has spent a lifetime Intending to do so, but because circumstances demand it.

Thinking about my last experience with the mushroom ally, when I was in that peak state where all rationality has gone out the window, I repeatedly asked "How do I direct my will?"

You're asking the wrong question. I cannot tell you the correct question in any linear fashion, but I can tell you that Will is often activated through the force of love – not the emotional type of love, but the love that transcends all reason and is what I have referred to as "the catalytic force of immortality," which is explored in a previous segment of this book.

Can the will be directed from inside time, from inside the human avatar? Or is it always something that you have no direct control over? I can will myself to evolve, because it is my will, but I can't will my bookcase to lift itself up and fly across the room just for the hell of it. So how would I direct it onto the bookcase?

Unless you had some *reason* to throw your Will at the bookcase, you might as well light a candle and pray for a flock of angels to descend upon the bookcase. The Will is a force like no other. It is not the common definition of "willpower" or any trivial mind game. It is the power to literally move mountains, or attain immortality. Not only do you have to want it enough, you have to have a *reason*. (Love is often that reason.)

Rather than waste time attempting to tell you about the Will, I'm going to suggest that you examine your Intent first and foremost. Determine what you *really* want to do. If that Intent is then focused over a period of time (no one can say how long) the Will may either cooperate in gaining your desire, or it will remain silent. My guess is that many seekers try to coerce the Will into action because they lack the motivation or ability to activate the living force of Intent (without which, there is *no* Will).

There are no "what ifs" or "whys" or even "hows." The Will cannot be understood through logical, rational, or scientific means. It can only be experienced. It comes at its own time and place, or not at all. The reason I have not written more extensively about this is that it cannot be written about extensively. Chase it, it runs. Catch it, it vanishes.

If you are trying to reason out the will, you are on a snipe hunt and you are the one holding the bag while simultaneously chasing your tail.

Meditate or Dis-Integrate

What follows is an excerpt from a conversation with an apprentice in 2002. I am often asked about meditation and assimilation and "Why oh why is it so important to sit in the dark silence with myself when I'd much rather be watching *The Big Bang Theory* or wasting time on Facebook?" This excerpt stemmed from one such dialog.

———

Once the commitment to the journey is made, it becomes mandatory to find the internal silence in order to listen to the voice of the Other. You are not special nor exempt from the process. If you think you are, it only illustrates how little you have learned, for without the gnostic connection to the Other, you are only a fragment of yourself, wandering and lost in some bedroom community of the dayshine world, and so it goes until one fine night you wake up dead while your Other stands on the edge of the abyss and weeps for your ignorant arrogance, and that is simply that.

The fool who believes he already knows everything can learn nothing.

What is it you are hoping to accomplish through this process? What is your goal into infinite eternity?

There is nothing particularly wrong or even confining with a physical body. It depends largely how that body is organized, energetically speaking. Tonight I am made of moon pixels and fairy dust, scattered matter of eternity.

112

Tomorrow, I will be a falling leaf or stray snowflake, always changing, but never dying. My *I-Am* may stand on the red sands of Mars or cavort with dead shamans in the underworld where the River Styx has its source and its terminal emptying into the endless ocean.

> *To be eternal is to be beyond the reach of death, beyond the ability to undo oneself. It is to be the mind and body of all the gods.*

It is my nature to be somewhat human and so that is what I normally choose to project. I enjoy life and so I reflect the living, see? I am all those things at all times. It is merely a matter of where I might choose to focus my awareness that will determine what I am. But I am always *I-Am*.

As long as you are within human manifestation, you will be human in your feelings. Unnatural control of those feelings is as dangerous as allowing the feelings to control you. Awareness is the razor's edge between light and dark, between love and hate, between day and night. Fall too far into the darkness, there can be no perception of light. Fall too far into the light, it will blind you. It is the amount of tension on the string that makes a beautiful sound or a discordant noise.

The path toward completing this evolution can *only* be based on action, which is why so few ever succeed.

Unless you intend to devote at least 20 minutes to meditation at a any one time, it is not really worth getting started. Normally, it requires an hour. More is better. Should it be daily? It should be *continual*. If it is a chore, you are doing it wrong. Your evolution must be a chosen joy, not a drudgery to be endured.

Where this journey is concerned, you will get out of it what you put into it. If you put 20 minutes a day into it, that is all you will get back. If it *is* your life, it will be your *eternal* life, yes? How can I stress to you that meditation is not an option

113

on a list of multiple choices? It is the assimilation of all you have learned. If you have not put the pieces together, the brute with the scythe will be happy to devour them just as they are.

When I am with the One(s) I love, we do not need to speak, for there is nothing to say. It is said and expressed in the falling star. It is known through the song of the owl in the distance. In the end, all that is real is love. This is the communion of gnosis, the conjoining of shared awareness which can only be achieved and accessed through the assimilated silence at the heart of every human heart.

You are at an advanced stage of the journey when your intent *must* begin to guide your actions. If you intend this evolution, meditation as assimilation should be a desirable alternative to ongoing distraction. If it is your Intent to Do this, it is important to begin looking at how you live on a daily basis. Have you assimilated the journey into your *I-Am* or are they still separate and fragmented items to be picked up and discarded on a whim?

It could be said that the body is a bubble sent to the surface when consciousness takes its first breath. But it is that very breathing and the creation of the bubble that gives the Other some idea of where to begin. It follows the bubbles. Without them, without the mortal self, the Other has no motivation, and though it has existence, that existence is without cohesion. It is by learning the nature of breathing that the bubbles eventually become only a byproduct and not the vessel of consciousness itself.

Apathy

One of the darkest truths of the darker teachings is that you *will* lose interest in the path.

I'm sure you're waiting for me to add, "...unless you do this or that" or "...until this or that occurs to bring you back in alignment."

Unfortunately, you will lose interest in the path and there is very little to be done about it other than to be constantly renewing your commitment with the awareness that if you *don't* seduce your immortal Other, he will find better things to do, and like an animal left unfed, he will return to the wild where you may see him peeking at you from the midnight from time to time, though his appearances will be less and less until, eventually, he will disappear altogether.

Damn, Mikal got up on the wrong side of the coffin this morning, you might think. Perhaps that is true. Perhaps it is just how you console yourself when you realize you are still human with human failings and human needs and human excuses for purely human behavior.

Why do humans lose interest so quickly? *Do* they lose interest, or am I just harping on the negative to scare you out of your complacency?

Essentially, humans are fickle fuckers. They chase rainbows for awhile (usually in their late teens and early 20s), but when the rainbow remains always in the distance (as muses and rainbows are wont to do), they declare sour grapes and move on to some other rainbow. But by the time they have chased a few, they tend to realize that rainbows are made of pixels of light and drizzle, and since light and drizzle don't make for something to be held in the hand or placed like a trophy on the mantle, rainbows are generally disregarded from that point forward, while the (former) seeker chooses to knuckle down, get with The Program, and put one foot in front of the other, straight on to the grave. "It's the responsible thing to do after all, and all that nonsense about immortality and the Other is just a fairy tale I told myself when I was young and irresponsible and rebelling against the world."

It's all but inevitable.

Unless you are the 1% of the 1% who have within yourself the ability to dismantle The Program, you will lose interest in the path. Sooner rather than later. You will tell yourself that Mikal is a liar and immortality is a fanciful fiction, and the Other is a muse who can never be caught. Maybe you will even believe it and never look back in that obsidian mirror where the night that never ends mocks you with vague but vanishing memories of the fire you felt when the Other was creeping around in the shadows, leaving notes of gnosis on the pillow of your Dreaming, and you stood psychically naked and mortally terrified at 3 a.m., knowing it was all real, feeling the essence of eternity swirling all around you, penetrating you like a lover, embracing you with all the love and forbidden passion the universe could possibly contain.

You will glance askance at those memories a time or two... and then, like a phantom, you will be gone. From the path. From the Other. From your Self.

What to do? Where's the happy ending? Where's the 5-minute-meditation that will make it all come rushing back?

Sorry to say, there is no cure for this syndrome. There is only you and your mirror and whatever unbending Intent you can summon. There is no magical ritual to keep your passion at a peak. There are no guardians or allies or mentors who can kick you in the ass to keep you focused. There isn't even the Other, unless that is your long-term, relentless commitment.

Intent is built on Intent.

The only thing you have is that awareness. And the absolute certainty of what happens if you *don't* rekindle those embers whenever you see them flickering toward ash and extinction. Do it or die. There is nothing in between but the in-between, and it's no place you want to be.

All That We See or Seem...

By believing passionately in something that still does not exist, we create it. The nonexistent is whatever we have not sufficiently desired.

~Nikos Kazantzakis

Why would imagination exist if not for us to dream into being that which did not exist before we imagined it?

Certain branches of quantum science postulate that anything we can imagine then exists wholly and absolutely. The thought is the thing. However, in the dayshine world, we have 7 billion people telling us that isn't so – and so the thing imagined exists and, simultaneously, does not exist, depending on the perception of the individual. Schrödinger's cat – dead and alive simultaneously.

It's interesting to observe that we now live in what might be called a *Star Trek* world. Many are too young to remember the original series, but it was a cornucopia of imagination and wonder. Of course, The Real World was quick to point out that talking computers were scientifically impossible. Enthusiastic seekers were told that communicators were a manifestation of fantasy, not reality. If man were meant to fly, he'd have starships. And so forth.

Now? The *Enterprise's* central computer would be obsolete even compared to desktop PCs of 10 years ago, let alone the super-fast models rolling off the line now. Communicators? We have cell phones that would have kept Captain Kirk and Mr. Spock out of a lot of trouble back in those days. My strong suspicion is that we even have warp drive and other so-called alien technology, but that's another conspiracy theory for another day.

We are being told that the singularity[22] will become a reality by 2045. Physical immortality is also slated for the same year – though it will only be viable for newborns and those still invitro, so the rest of you true seekers need to stir your imaginations and do it the old fashioned way. You have to *be* immortal before you will know how to *become* immortal.

As usual, science is catching up to what mystics have known throughout the ages.

The trick to Becoming is wanting it enough, and imagining it into manifestation through action.

Blasphemy!

Christians have basically spouted to the world that their path is the only path to God/Enlightenment for 2100 years and counting. Some have even said that "vampirism" is a knock-off and perversion of the sacraments, transubstantiation notwithstanding. Just for the record what do you say on this?

Christianity is only one of more than a thousand religions and a million deviations. Every religion claims to possess "the one true god," and so the followers of any religion are programmed to believe their way is the *only* way. The moment they adopt that belief, they lose any hope of *Realizing* that the one true god is the one in the mirror. Most Christian sects also teach that even thinking such a thing is the unpardonable sin – blasphemy. That particular teaching has turned the church into the very devil it rails against, because when religion robs a person of their personal power (the ability and the right to transform/transcend/transmogrify), the church has become the slayer of souls; and most immortals are saints by comparison.

---

[22]The Singularity: A hypothetical state wherein human consciousness will be embedded into technological devices, achieving what some believe is a form of techno-immortality.

The darker teachings recognize that religion is one of the most vile institutions on Earth, because the vast majority of organized religions are all about disempowering their followers and turning them into doe-eyed zombies handing out flowers at the airport or running around the country on bicycles spewing rhetoric that not only falsifies reality, but actively seeks to convert others into the brotherhood of consensual lies.

When analyzing the prevailing myth, Jesus himself was quite probably a vampire. As I've stated elsewhere, my personal definition of a vampire is someone who has transcended the mortal state and recognizes themselves as a citizen of the universe rather than a transient visitor on Planet Earth. If the myths of Jesus are anywhere near true (no way to know), it's clear that he was 1) a shamanic spirit who reasoned things out for himself, up to and including the art of transmogrification; and 2) he was able to "turn" others.

It's *how* he turned others that may bear some examination. "Eat my body, drink my blood, and you will never die." Sounds like a vampire to me – or at least it sounds like what most people think of when they think of vampires. But what lies beyond those words? I've said much the same to some of my apprentices (yes, I do enjoy the sin of blasphemy), and what it really means to a true seeker is simply this:

Eat my body: My body is energy – the immortalis-animus manifested. Take that awareness into yourself, and you will never die, for the power of the immortalis-animus is transformative.

Drink my blood: My blood is Knowledge – the living stream of awareness through which the seeker may access the voice of gnosis, silent knowing, the immortal Other.

And you will never die: As the seeker takes into himself the body and blood of the immortalis-animus (not any entity but the living *essence* of Life) the seeker becomes an eternal being.

Now... there are at least 10,000 ways anyone could quite intentionally misconstrue my words. Just as I'm certain they misconstrued the alleged words of the alleged Jesus. As the old saying goes, to someone who has experienced this, no further explanation is necessary. To someone who has not, no further explanation is possible. And so it all becomes a churning miasma of words, which are always only fodder for misunderstanding and erroneous conclusions.

It often seems to me that the religions that preach love are the least likely to practice it, the least likely to become the reflection of the God they claim to worship. With that said, how do the vampire teachings fit into the scheme of things?

The reason most religious fanatics refuse to walk in love and become "god" is because the church figured out long ago that people who actually *do* this no longer need the church. Follow the money. *Always* follow the money.

I would say that the vampire teachings are much closer to the truth, more ancient, and that Christianity and other religions are a bastardization of that truth (specifically referring to rituals and dogma). When I use the word "truth" here, what I'm referring to is what might be called the milieu that lies at the bottom of the rabbit hole. The only way to Know those truths is through the art of silent knowing.

Ultimately the Other is the vessel of eternal awareness – not just eternal, but ubiquitous throughout space-time and beyond. The seeker who truly connects with the Other has the potential to connect with truth.

The problem is that Christianity (and most other religions) teach that humans are born with a soul and are therefore already immortal in some sense of the word. Christianity, for

120

example, teaches that one will either go to heaven or hell depending on their actions, and whether or not the individual dies in a state of grace. At the *core*, there is some minor truth to this, but the church has injected itself into the middle of the equation, and made the doctrine that all one must do to be saved is to believe.

Nothing could be further from the truth.

If salvation exists at all, it is through the creation of the Other – and this is not something that happens by default. It is what has been called "The Great Work," and it is the work of a lifetime in the sense that it requires the examination of the self (who are you?); the elimination of the programs that bind you to your mortality (such as the belief that one must be saved by an extant deity); and the willful surrender that occurs when the seeker ultimately embraces the totality of herself.

> *A voodoo priestess once told Wade Davis: You white people go to church and talk about God. In voodoo, we dance in the Temple and become God!*

True seekers project the Other into the infinite, and become god – immortal, eternal, true. Dancing not required, but *highly* recommended. Above all else, a path should have heart and alignment with the seeker's predilections. Blind devotion and the mumbled prayers of the faithful won't save anyone from the inside of a coffin.

What Holds it All Together?

Why am I finding it so difficult to interact with my fellow humans? It's as if they are literally aliens, or I am a different species. Thing is – I feel like I'm being absorbed just by virtue of constant exposure.

The humans are difficult because they are so lost and therefore, by definition, completely insane. Yet we often find ourselves loving them as well. It's as I have said before: there can be no altruism. It leads to an overwhelming and impossible responsibility for others, and you and your *own I-Am* run the high risk of getting trampled in the chaos.

And yet, there is that interconnectedness between everything that makes it impossible to ignore the antics of others. Too often, even those immortals who choose to play the human games again either get carried back into the wretched human trap of forgetting ourselves, or become loners and walk the endless beauty of the nightroads for Time unending, hoping yet not hoping to find treasures of meaning along the way, hoping yet not hoping for love. There is no avoidance of this, only knowing that you cannot make the human world other than what it is, you can only make yourself that which you long for, your desire manifested, your self whole.

When you hear the wind crying over your house, that is me, weeping bitterly for the human world. When you hear the rain laughing on your rooftops, that is me, laughing at the wonder that it even exists, that we can do this, that gnosis is a word invented by my people thousands of years ago and some, and so it goes. I am real, yet I dart around your house like some shadow to you, barely there. But that is only because you are in the human world and still seeing the shadows on Plato's cave. That world is made of shadows, and the storm of perception breaks through only when you realize that everything you think is unreal is not, and everything you think is real is not.

Once you realize this, once you are an immortal prowling winter streets in search of treasures not yet found (and secretly hoping to find none so you can go home as empty as you left, so your sleep is silent) you gain an understanding that you are the *only* soul fiber that holds it all together, and your mind functions as the thread within the weave and then you know that it all falls apart when you do; and that you must not ever stop or the No-thing will win and then the universe will have to start from scratch again with a word or a shudder or a spontaneous ohm.

No Going Back

I once had an apprentice who was very close to transmogrification when she chose to throw it all over her shoulder and run screaming back to the consensual world. I was never 100% sure of *what* sent her running back to the matrix, though I strongly suspect it was an underlying self-loathing she was never able to eliminate, combined with a general laziness of mind/body/spirit. In the final analysis, she didn't love herself enough to keep going. She had no clue of this, but I could *see* it through her actions and in her energetic field.

An evolved individual is a *healthy* individual (in spirit even if not always in physical form), and she couldn't handle the responsibility that comes with being Whole. I had told her shortly before she departed that I would not be able to teach her anything further. Reason being – there is a point in the darker teachings where some of the knowledge can actually be harmful (life-threatening, in fact) if the seeker hasn't developed a sufficiently sound foundation of self-awareness. If the seeker is still attached to the programs but only *pretending* to be free of them, the darker teachings have been known to send them screaming into the abyss – not because they are particularly scary but because they can literally unravel the dayshine world to such an extent that the seeker may find herself in what can only be termed a state of irreversible madness. When what someone blindly believes comes into direct confrontation with evidence to the contrary, a massive shift of the assemblage point is inevitable – and often irreversible.

The problem is that when one truly transmogrifies, it's not as easy to undo the process as you might think.

Why would someone ever want to undo it?

Humans are fickle by nature. They may embrace something with great passion one day only to toss it away the next.

mortals grow up
grow old
move away.
too often
they forget to pack
their dreams
and so the king
shivers in an empty driveway
pining after taillights,
another abandoned pet.

With extreme age comes extreme grief, loss, pain. Many (most) simply cannot handle that over a period of decades, centuries, millennia. As a mortal, humans move along in what amounts to a timeline shared with others. Friends and lovers grow old and die more or less at the same time (assuming a relatively kind universe). With immortals, there is a heavy gravity that comes with watching those we love grow old and die while we continue on into a future where change is not only unavoidable, but altogether necessary for one's survival.

124

It is when immortals cling to the past that they can no longer face the future. And so a few would rather return to the matrix for that juicy steak rather than live in "the real world" of their own making.

> *This path chooses you. You do not choose it. If it is in your blood, you will know. If it isn't, it will eat you alive from the inside out and toss the bones over its shoulder. There are no exceptions – not even for those who believe they are entitled to an exception. It. Is. Forever.*

We Are All Mad Here

These finely mad fools (of which I consider myself one) are able to function in the real world, whereas those who are <u>truly</u> mad need some manner of keeper. In fact, I think seekers <u>have</u> to be finely mad in order to take this path on at all. But what <u>is</u> a good definition of 'truly mad'?

Being truly mad would mean not having the ability to navigate the world at large. Some would-be seekers like to think that madness is an attribute, but in the long run, if one cannot navigate *this* world, they will hardly be able to navigate (or even create) the Otherworld, which we might also call vampireland.

I'd like to know more about the ability of the program to re-enslave someone who has freed himself from it. You've said before, "The only way to kill an immortal is to make him believe he is mortal." Is that the same thing? If so, how is it avoided?

I know seekers who have stood at the brink of immortality, then fallen into the abyss because of a single intruding thought that whispers, "All things die. Don't be ridiculous. Step away from the precipice of freedom and come back to the fold where you are loved and protected and there are cookies and warm milk."

How to avoid it? By knowing the tactics and the *intent* of the program. To the consensus, you are a cog in the wheel of society, and as such you are greatly valued. The consensus feeds on you by sucking your life away – *by making you believe you are irreversibly mortal.* This is not metaphor or allegory. It is one of the most basic and brutal truths you will ever learn – not something anyone can teach you, but something you will see when you *see* the world as it is rather than how you have been taught to believe.

The consensus even has its own voice, which you experience as the doubting and accusatory and debilitating drone of the internal dialog, which, aside from playing old Neil Diamond songs over and over in your head to distract you, thrives on tearing you down until you have only enough energy to keep going, a cog in service to the machine, but a machine that serves no purpose other than its own existence, of which it is not even remotely aware.

Such is the irony of the human condition.

The machine is a gestalt of all living beings it has consumed, yet even with so much energy and awareness in its possession, it has not a single gram of consciousness of its own. It is nothing more than a gullet and a mouth full of teeth, devouring everything in its path, not to survive as an evolving entity, but simply to prevent the evolution of other living beings, and exterminate those who try to get in its way. After all, we're all just bricks in the wall, no?

126

The only way to avoid this is to always be aware of it at the most fundamental level. Sounds simple, but isn't. The machine has the most clever ways of invading the seeker's intent – often masquerading as what it will try to convince you is curiosity, but is really just an attempt to argue with Truth. Cleverness is an attribute of the machine, and you will see it in a lot of wannabes.

There was once a member of the Immortal Spirit forum who thought it was clever to find loopholes and fallacies in the concept of immortality, and while I do encourage questioning everything, there comes a point when the questioning is no longer for the purpose of gaining knowledge, but becomes an attempt to undermine any concept that exists outside the comfort zone of the status quo.

Avoiding being pulled back into the machine's hungry maw after one has defeated it is also a matter of realizing that its very intent to pull you back *in* means there *is* an "out." Once that fully sinks in, the machine begins to lose power over you, but it is a master of pulling you back in. How it does this is dependent on your own currency. If you have a loving family, it may strike there – creating strife or illness or a situation in which *you* are desperately *needed* to deal with this or that situation.

If you are a creative individual, the machine may work overtime figuring out ways to keep you from doing the things you love. It is almost never a frontal assault, but sneaks up from behind. If you have defeated most of these attacks and freed yourself from these imposed (but also imagined) responsibilities, the machine may begin to attack you directly – health issues, old belief systems resurfacing. There are literally an infinite number of ways it will try to reinstall itself, rather like an old computer trying to reboot until, eventually, it reverts to the blue screen of death, and only then are you finally free.

It only takes a lifetime. Or ten. Ten thousand?

To Breed or Not to Breed

I always wanted children, but a lot of the reading I've done about spiritual evolution seems to say that children may be a bad idea for a warrior-seeker. What's your take on this?

In all probability, most will not like my answer. Nothing new there. While I would love to tell you the usual platitudes – "Children are a blessing!" "Children are a gift from Spirit!" "Children will *enhance* your spiritual journey rather than detract from it!" – I have sworn an oath to be truthful according to my own observations and experiences.

That being said, I can only say with tongue firmly in cheek, "Children are best served warm, with a hint of salt and ketchup."

"OMG! Is Mikal advocating cannibalism? I can't even cook!"

No, Mikal is not advocating cannibalism. Mikal is attempting to tell you the truth about how children integrate with seekers on a path toward evolution. The simple answer: *Generally* speaking, they *don't*.

Now don't call in the storm troopers. Children are all fine and good. Some grow up into fine doctors, lawyers, and leaders. Others grow up into meth heads, morons, and may even become President of the United States.

Children are a full time job all by themselves, and tend to require almost constant supervision for several years. Yes, that can be relegated to nanny or a daycare facility, but if that's the case, do you *really* want children, or do you just like the *idea* of children?

Anything you truly desire requires a commitment of time and energy, children and the path most of all. Yes, it is *possible* to have it both ways. But it is seldom how things work out. I've known excellent seekers who start out on the path with fire in their eyes, only to wake up one day to the realization that they now have 2.5 children, a house in the suburbs with a large mortgage, two gas-guzzling SUVs, and a dog that craps on the rug at least twice daily. Braces for the middle child. Therapy for the eldest (and both parents). Private school for the entire brood. Cell phones and video game consoles as they grow up a bit. Rehab. Bail. A good lawyer...

And so it goes. Of course, maybe *you* are blessed with The Perfect Little Angel(s), but even if that turns out to be the case, what you discover is that all your time and energy go to the children and seldom is anything left over at the end of the day for yourself. I'm not saying it *can't* be done. I'm asking if *you* have the stamina and the resources it's going to take. Will *you* have the time, energy and interest left over for *your* journey, or will you find yourself lost in the miasma of mumps and measles, core math and spelling bees, horny teenage boyfriends and all the other trials and tribulations that go into the proper care and feeding of this lifeform that starts out as a cute little infant and quickly grows into an energy vampire of epic proportions.

"OMG – did Mikal just call children energy vampires?"

Yes. Mikal did.

It's not their fault. It's just the nature of the beast, and if *you* don't have the expensive ingredients it's going to take to get from zero to 18 years, then you really have to stop and ask yourself which you want *more*. Many – *most!* – find that they really do want children. It's ingrained into the human organism from the time they are old enough to hold a Barfing Baby Betty. In fact, most cultures actually frown on those who choose *not* to take on the responsibility of being a parent, and so there is the added pressure from friends, family and – especially – religious organizations, to breed like happy rabbits until the womb falls exhausted onto the floor and Viagra can no longer cure the drooping cuke.

"Mikal is an asshole! Children are the future! Children are my immortality!"

And therein lies one of *the* most dangerous belief systems, and one that will be the death of you if you're not careful. Sure, children may carry forth your name and your bloodline (but if you still think those things *matter*, you have not yet mastered the art of *seeing*). If you're lucky, maybe your offspring will even take with them some of the Knowledge you bestow on them.

> **But children don't make you immortal anymore than a radioactive spider bite gives you super-powers.**

The real issue – and this cannot be stressed strongly enough – is that children are not like puppies. You can't leave them locked in the house while you to go work. You can't put them out to pee while you go about your business. Just when you get into a light meditative state, they *will* come knocking on your door – whether asking for a bedtime story or to report a mysterious fire in their bedroom sparked by aliens or evil elves (because of course they would *never* play with matches) – and by the time you have calmly handled all of *their* crises, dawn is breaking and you're an old man, and even though you truly love the little tykes with all that remains of your heart, most simply will not have the physical or emotional endurance to pursue the path *and* raise children.

I wish it were different. And it *can* be. But that's the exception and not the rule. How does it play out for *you*?

In some esoteric writings, it is even suggested that just the act of *having* children leaves an energetic hole in the parents. The energy required to create the spark of Life has to come from somewhere – and that is from the mind/body/spirit of both the mother and the father. Many seers can accurately tell not only *if* someone has had children, but how many – based on the number of holes in the energy body. Some say these holes can be healed over time; others vehemently disagree, claiming the holes are permanent and irreversible.

Whatever the ultimate truth might be with regard to the physical and metaphysical effects producing children has on body of the self and the Other, one thing is certain: children are a massive investment of time, energy, and love; and so is the path. A lot of seekers have truly believed they can have both. A rare few have succeeded. Most don't.

Choose wisely.

How Do I Know This Path is for Me?

The only way to know is by how you feel. Most seekers feel on track when they are doing what some call pathwork. That might mean meditating, reading, researching, or engaging in some practice. But the real test is how you feel when you are performing the chores of your ordinary life – going to work, cooking, working on the car, dealing with the tyrants in your life. If you stop and examine your feelings during these activities, and you find that you feel *off* track or not in tune with your Other, then the problem is one of conflict – a line in the sand drawn between your ordinary life and your path.

The key to becoming self-integrated is remembering these words: "Those who succeed are not only *on* the path, they *are* the path." If you are not mining your Intent at all times, even when doing activities that might otherwise be considered mundane, then you are not approaching the path from a 100% commitment. This is common among those new to the teachings, and may persist for years. But once the seeker begins to self-integrate, he will begin to see much greater progress and may feel imbued with a sense of well-being and increased awareness even when performing the most mundane duties. The trick is maintaining awareness in everything you are doing – not just an idle thought, but an active force which begins to work in the background, guiding your actions even without your conscious awareness.

Stalk yourself ruthlessly. How do you *feel*? Look at what you are doing and particularly, look at the mindset with which you are approaching that activity. If you are at work, for example, feeling like you must get home so you can do pathwork, then you have identified your nemesis. It isn't *work* that's stopping you. It's your belief that you can't be doing pathwork *while* at work.

Awareness of mindset is crucial.

The path is not what you <u>do</u>, it is who you <u>are</u>.

If you're feeling annoyed that you're not on the path at that moment, it's because you *aren't* on the path at that moment. You are still divided, fragmented. When your Intent is active, there is no difference between being at work, in a cubicle, or on top of a mountain in Tibet.

The Dark Enlightenment

What actually happens when you become enlightened? Do you grow wings or something? And how do you know you have gained enough knowledge to become enlightened? What happens if you die before becoming enlightened? And if you did have the chance to become enlightened, wouldn't you simply become like god?

You do not become a god. (There is no such thing.)

You do not grow wings. (They are unwieldy and prone to molting.)

You do not become omniscient. (Though you do have access to gnosis.)

You do not automatically become a blissful ninny. {Many enlightened individuals are darklings.)

It's not a matter of gathering information. Knowledge cannot be gathered, but may only be attained through direct personal experience.

What happens when you become enlightened is that you simply *see* things as they are. Becoming enlightened removes your comfort zones by no longer allowing you to lie to yourself.

Intent + Action = Manifestation
Undoing the Myths Surrounding "The Law of Attraction"

Belief is a fool's paper sword. Believing you are immortal doesn't *make* you immortal. But it is a step toward undoing the belief that tells you that you are mortal. Belief can be a tool, but also a dangerous trap. Like everything else, it is a double-edged blade and one must know which side of the blade to use in which circumstances.

Many students of "The Secret" have ended up on my couch. Not that I have a couch, of course. I'm hardly a therapist. More of a truthsayer often accused of being a soothsayer. But no matter.

Why do proponents of "The Secret" end up on my website and in my forums? Because wishing, hoping or believing in something doesn't make it so. The equation goes something like this:

Intent + Action = Manifestation

Intent may originally be comprised of certain elements of belief – a belief that immortality is possible may lead to the Intent to attain it – but Intent is a moving force unto itself. And yet, without action, there can be no real manifestation. This is why seekers go through a variety of practices, some of which will become their regular doings, others of which will fall by the way as the journey progresses and evolves.

What we read and learn can have extreme value, but only when it is put to *action*.

As for *The Secret* – I don't believe there *is* a secret. But apparently a lot of people *do* and have gotten hooked into some fanciful notion that wishing for something will bring it to them. Unfortunately, what I have observed in these people is that they were set up to fail – whether *they* knew it or not, and whether the writers of *The Secret* knew it or not.

The law of attraction is essentially caca de toro, particularly as it was put forth in *The Secret*. Those who think they can wish for something and have it appear are suffering from the cognitive bias that tells them either 1) they are very, very special; or 2) Jesus loves you. Either delusion will only prevent the apprentice from doing the work required to manifest intent.

There are no shortcuts.

There is an art and practice known as creative visualization – and I can say from experience and observation that it does have positive outcomes. Sometimes. But *only* when the equation at the top of this section is put into practice. If you're visualizing a shiny new car, it might occur to you that you will need to have the *means* to facilitate the end. You might have to get a job or at the very least enter a sweepstakes or go to a local casino and invest $50K to win a car valued at approximately $15K. How you *do* it is up to you. But I can virtually guarantee you won't wake up tomorrow morning to find a BMW parked in your driveway with a big bow on top and a note that reads, "Because you wished for it."

You're not that special. Neither am I. Neither is anyone else on this planet with the possible exception of some entitled princess who has never worked a day in her life, but still manages to have every little thing fall into her lap as if by magic. It *isn't* magic, of course. It's just a byproduct of being born into privilege. Nothing wrong with that, but it isn't a recipe for success where this path is concerned. In fact, I've known a couple of princes and princesses who have consciously *denounced* their life of privilege in order to experience first hand what it means to *manifest* what is desired as opposed to having it handed to them on a silver spoon. After all, silver spoons are often laced with poison, or at the very least, with expectations and obligations. There are no free rides. Certainly not where this path is concerned.

So if you have fallen into the trap of thinking you can hope for something and draw little pictures of it in your wishbook, by all means, carry on. But rest assured that *wishing* for immortality won't get you past the starting gate any more than pining after Prince Charming will bring him to your bed.

One of the first tenets of sorcery is this: Action is the interface between what-I-desire and what-I-*Will*. It isn't what you *want* that turns the wheel. It is Willful *force* applied in the form of action.

> *How does this apply to the creation of the Other? What form of action can we really take to bring the twin into manifestation?*

If you want to meet someone who doesn't exist, you first have to create them. How will you go about it? This is where chaos magick can be helpful as a tool, particularly in the beginning. If you aren't familiar with chaos magick, I recommend the works of Peter J. Carroll. There are also other good books on chaos magick, just be careful to avoid bliss ninny new age jibber-jabber.

If you like a particular actor or actress, pattern your Other on that person's physical attributes at first. Just be *very* careful not to confuse the actor with the being you are creating (or, more precisely, *manifesting*). If you have ever felt that inexplicable longing in the center of your being, focus that energy into your visualizations. Write a sigil. Write a poem. Write a song.

Create.

That is the force of *action*.

The goal here is to harness the energy of your *desire* and channel it from visualization into *Realization*. The hardest battle one faces is the voice of the internal dialog, informing you that this is foolish, it cannot be done, it is silly, impossible, and you are wasting time that would be better spent in church. The only way to combat that voice is to focus on the ache/hurt/want/need that gnaws at you from nowhere and everywhere, and whispers promises of love, joy, and, most of all, *Wholeness,* that is possible when mortal self and immortal Other unite. It is not some trite and meaningless one night stand. It is not even an epic love affair worthy of a Shakespearean sonnet. It is instead the incalculable power and eternal presence of the singularity of consciousness – the spark that ignites the immortal flame.

Sometimes you simply have to *do* that which has never been done – not in some petty display of power, but because the soul itself is empty and alone if you don't.

It is the most selfish thing you can do. And that is why you *must* do it... for your Self. For *ever.*

Duel With Your Dualism

Time itself is an illusion in which you are trapped like a reflection caught in a mirror.

The only thing to do about it is to know who you are. And that often begins by knowing who and what you are *not.* Without ever realizing it, you have become a machine efficiently programmed by The Program itself. How it occurs is obvious only in hindsight, when you stand on the far side of the bridge and look over your shoulder to see how the bridge was built. What you don't know is that you are not really your*Self.* You are an unremarkable puzzle crafted by friends and family, teachers and peers. You are the sum total of *their* beliefs, and probably have very few (if any) of your own.

> *Until you summon your cohesion and bring forth your individuation, you are little more than a puzzle where all the pieces are the same color – a patchwork conglomeration of the beliefs of your programmers.*

How to know the difference between who *you* are and who you have been *told* to *be*?

Challenge yourself to a duel. One of you is your programming. The other you is what you yourself have experienced directly. Look at something. Anything. Let's say you look at a stack of books sitting on a table. *The Bible. The Collected Works of William Shakespeare. Harry Potter. A Child's Garden of Verse. Illusions. National Audubon Field Guide for North American Mushrooms. See Spot Run. Teachings of the Immortals. Fun With Flags.*

Whether you are aware of it or not, you have beliefs about each and every book, depending on the source and depth of your programming. Even if you are completely unfamiliar with the subject matter, some of the books will give you a feeling of hope. Others may bring despair. But unless you have actually *read* the books in question, you are responding solely on your programming.

If the Bible makes you feel safe or secure, it is only because you have been *told* you should feel God's love. If *Harry Potter* makes you shrink away, it's because you've been programmed to have that reaction to anything potentially mystical. If Shakespeare makes you feel heavy and oppressed, it's not because Shakespeare is an old fuddy-duddy, it's because you have been *told* to have that reaction to the classics (because we all know you haven't read it).

And so it goes. You have no personal experience with any of these books, but you find yourself drawn toward one or instinctively pushing it away. Ask yourself why. Find out what your programmed self believes and why he believes it.

Then shoot the bastard in the head. (You just won the duel.)

But now you are alone in the wilderness of wonderfulness with not a clue as to where to go or who you are, not even who you might *want* to be. This is really where the journey begins – when you stop blindly believing all of those fast-talkers inside your head and get a grip on your real self (and no, that self is not found in betwixt your nethers). When you can look at that same stack of books and feel *nothing*, you have made some progress in the direction of getting rid of some of your programming. But it's not just about books. It's everything you *think* you know about life, but really only believe.

I had an intense discussion with someone recently on the subject of, "If you don't vote, you can't complain." While the sentiment expressed may have some validity (to the one making the statement), the reality is a bit different. Complaining and voting are not conjoined at the hip, and doing either one doesn't make you a better or worse person. You really don't have a civic duty. What you have (*hopefully*) is common sense. If you find a *reason* to vote, then do it. If you don't, you have no reason to bother. All elections are already decided long before they go to polls, and if you think otherwise it's only because you've been programmed to believe your vote Matters with a big capital M. News flash – it really doesn't, but I don't even *want* to convince you of that, because then you are only believing *me* instead of learning to *see* it for yourself.

If you don't know who you are, at least take a look in the mirror and figure out who you are *not*. If something causes you to recoil or to rejoice, ask yourself why. Eventually, you may whittle away all the bullshit that's been heaped onto you by the world and the culture and the society, and if you're extremely lucky, you just might find your Other gazing back at you, asking, "Where the hell have you been? I've been waiting."

Don't wait too long.

You said, " When you can look at that same stack of books and feel <u>nothing</u>, you have made some progress in the direction of getting rid of some of your programming." Would you consider this apathy, detachment, something in between? Looking at a Bible doesn't bother me in and of itself; it's just a *book. However, it is an object that reminds me of all the atrocities, large and small, that have been committed in the name of it and its god. Removing the feelings associated with those memories from the act of seeing or reading a Bible would be difficult for me.*

When I say you feel nothing what I mean is that you have no reaction, which is an attribute of detachment. I have no great love of the Bible either (to use your example) but I would not waste energy being attached to the atrocities committed in its name – because it is not in my power to change the past, and not heavily in my power to influence the future. It is possible to have awareness of something without feeling a need to do something about it. As an immortal, you would spend all of eternity attempting to correct the past, or simply feeling bad about it, rather than living in the moment.

Curiosity is normal for a seeker. The underlying task is to follow the path of *your* heart rather than getting caught up in the beliefs put onto you by others along the long and winding road. The problem *every* seeker faces is that these seemingly intrinsic beliefs about life, the universe and everything in between are *so* deep that most will honestly think they are your own conclusions. That is what kills you. That is what it is designed to do.

My original comments about dueling with your duality were prompted by a seeker who often asks why he can't seem to make any real progress on the path. To me, it is obvious – it is because he is so weighed down with the belief systems of *others* that he has no real identity of his own. Of course, most will choose to defend their current status quo rather than considering there is something beyond it. That, too, is what kills you.

I prefer this quote, which puts it all in perspective:

"None are more hopelessly enslaved than those who falsely believe they are free." (Goethe)

Stalking the Authentic Self

What about using psychedelics to stalk yourself? It was a common practice in the Castaneda books. What's your take on it? What about other types of drugs – cocaine, heroine, LSD?

If you want to experiment with self-stalking, there is really no need to go as far as hard drugs. In fact, there is every reason *not* to damage your mind, body, and spirit with cocaine, heroine, methamphetamines and the like You don't even *really* need psychedelics, but if you *do* decide to experiment with the mushroom ally, peyote, or the other traditional plant allies, I would strongly advise doing it *only* under the supervision of a master shaman. In the meantime, try these other ways to stalk yourself.

1. Pick a food you hate (or think you do) and eat nothing but that food one day.

2. Select a co-worker or classmate (depending on your age and maturity level) whom you really don't like and befriend them. This is generally a more long-term act of stalking that will give you a better idea of why you *think* you don't like so-and-so, and ultimately gives you a better insight into your own stubborn programs.

3. Go to a movie of a type you generally don't like. If you hate war movies, go to one. If you hate romantic comedies, go to one. Sit through it with an open mind.

4. If you are an atheist, go to a formal Catholic mass or other highly ritualized religious gathering.

5. If you are a religious person, jump off a cliff and ask God to save you. (No, *don't* really do this, but think about it – flip your thinking, in other words). What you will generally

discover in this experiment is that you are more of an atheist than you thought – you don't *really* believe God is going to save you, so your deprogramming needs some work.

6. Take a job for which you are over-qualified (assuming you aren't already asking "Would you like fries with that?"). If you are a stock broker, try working as a janitor for a week.

7. Put yourself in a situation that will require you to think on your feet in subtle ways. Example – go to a funeral of someone you didn't know. If someone asks, "How did you come to know The Dearly Departed," use your own connection to gnosis to come up with a plausible answer. If you blunder, you'll find out that you're not the hotshot you thought you were. If you succeed, it will give you a foundational knowledge of what *seeing* actually *feels* like. There are plenty of ways to do this experiment. Watch *Wedding Crashers* for some pointers.

All of these are just ways to shift your assemblage point without doing long-term damage to yourself. These are just ways of examining the foundation of your programming. No drugs required. Common sense *highly* recommended

Pushing The Boulder Uphill

Is evolution occurring more rapidly now than in the past?

In many ways, evolution is perhaps *more* difficult in these "modern times" than it was even 50 years ago or certainly 100 years ago. Though it could be perceived that humans had to work harder to survive, they were also much more tribal in nature, so the work was often divided in such a way that there was more spare time than you might think.

There weren't as many programs to overcome, nor were there as many distractions. The result was the people were actually more introspective. Many were conditioned by religion and therefore gave up their opportunity to evolve, but many others saw the illusion for what it was even then. Statistically speaking, I would say that a higher percentage evolved 300 years ago than in today's world. The main reason for that is, simply, technological distraction and the dumbing down of the human race.

We literally are born into knowledge and have almost everything at our disposal, which I postulate would reduce the time needed to assimilate and learn the knowledge required for transmogrification.

As a facilitator, I would say it's just the opposite. I can see why you would come to these conclusions, but I don't see any real evidence to support them. I sincerely wish it were otherwise. The reality is that most people have lost all interest. in matters of Spirit – they have traded their spare time for video games or internet surfing or dozens of other plug-ins to the techno-world rather than plugging into Spirit, so the end result is that fewer and fewer people even have any interest in the idea of immortality. They have been programmed to believe it doesn't exist, or that it will be handed to them in the form of "the singularity" in the year 2045, and so they have virtually no motivation to engage in The Work.

I see the illusion for what it is: a video game, the matrix, insert your own term. Does it make me crazy for seeing how crazy this all is? Why would a benevolent creator allow us to rationalize this much?

You've answered your own question. There is no benevolent creator. There is only the self. As I've said: Thou art god. Create yourself accordingly.

A few esoteric and shamanic traditions postulate that there is a "foreign installation" – something I've talked about elsewhere in this book, but which bears a closer examination. In the grand scheme of things, the foreign installation *does* exist – but it is the gestalt of *human* fears, programs, erroneous conclusions, and false belief systems.

Humans don't need aliens or gods to create a foreign installation. They are more than capable of doing that all by themselves.

Where is the Real Magic?

There is a vast misconception of what real magic actually is. It's not just about bringing money to yourself, as an example. It's not about getting women or men or sheep in your bed.

Real magic is about manipulating and channeling energy as a way to alter the matrix (the program, the consensus). Many real magicians are children who do not yet adhere to the rules of the consensus and so they are able to manipulate energy in ways no adult can comprehend (and few can even perceive).

Real magicians are plentiful – some know it, others don't.

> *Real magic is the key to immortality – for immortality is a state of being that exists outside the matrix, and which can be accessed through a shift of energy, an alteration of one's energetic structure from organic to inorganic.*

In olden days, this was referred to as alchemy. Unfortunately, the definition of alchemy nowadays generally refers to the transference of iron (or other ore) into gold through magical manipulations. But the real magician isn't concerned with gold or even money. She has all there is and all there will be... at her fingertips.

Health

There is nothing wrong with trying to maintain your health, but humans want to prolong their youth to immortality without even knowing it. At the end of the day, only rare individuals can actually go on a spiritual journey toward enlightenment. This path requires too much sacrifice and mental preparation.

What you are saying is very true, particularly in the early stages of the journey. And yet, what *seems* so hard really isn't... yet is... yet isn't. *("Mikal is talking in double-speak again.")*

What is really happening is that people are trying to make the shift from the flawed organic self to the perfected inorganic self. It isn't even really a shift of molecules or state of being. It is a shift of *awareness*, a shift from a belief that humans are mortal organics to a system of Knowledge that humans are comprised of the same starstuff as the immortal universe itself. The universe has always been here and always will be – in one form or another. It is not possible for it to be otherwise. You (all things) are part of that quantum matrix, intricately interwoven with the infinite hologram.

Once you truly *Know* this beyond all humanform doubts, you will have achieved the immortal condition – wherein death and time are illusions spawned by the antimatter antithesis of immortality. No actual words exist for this antimatter antithesis, and so it is most often referred to in the vernacular as, simply, death.

In the big picture, most humans strive toward their natural state – which is the state of energy at the quantum level. Perhaps the best name for *that* state is the singularity of consciousness.

Seekers are aware of the journey and give themselves a better opportunity to transcend the matrix with their awareness intact. Phantoms strive toward the same goal, but without awareness they run the high risk (almost an inevitability) that their individuality will be utterly obliterated at the moment of death. The difference, therefore, between the mortal and the immortal, is the difference between a singularity and a splatter-fest, the difference between cohesion and obliteration.

Without realizing it on any conscious level, people struggle to maintain their physical health and appearance of youth because they are attempting to emulate the immortal Other.

Terrified

Everything I thought was "me" is a lie. It's painful to admit and I keep returning to this lie as if it is the truth – when in reality it is the other way around. All this time I have been rebellious and stubborn and clung to these ideas, thinking they were what made up my heart. The problem is that the alleged "reality" is no more real than these – it is <u>all</u> falsehood. I used these fabricated ideas to drive my evolution and they were what got me onto this path. Did the Program find a way to take my path to freedom and twist it to suit its own agenda?

That scares me because that means absolutely nothing is me or my own. I recognize it is all conditioning since the day I was born, the result of chemical interactions, bad parenting, influences of women and friends, and the things that I read.

Am I to forsake physical beauty, things like music, power? Do all roads in the dayshine world lead to nothing? I have no idea why, but there is still some part of me that wants to try. Some need to remove all the falsehood. I am willing to give up these rebellious beliefs and comfort zones, as much as they scream in my head as I just type this – and I suppose that is how I know they are false. I just don't quite know what to replace them with.

What do I propel myself with if I can't trust anything in my head or my heart?

What you're expressing here is a state of mind that most seekers experience at several points in their journey. It's why I've always said that if you are going to destroy the programs (the foundation) on which your life has been built, you *must* have something to replace it with so you don't go tumbling headlong into the abyss.

It is things like beauty, music, poetry, prose, and anything exceptionally creative that may serve to bolster that new foundation. The greatest musicians, for example, are often rooted in mysticism. I'm thinking of Jim Morrison. Curt Kobain. Lots of others.

What I would recommend is too simple, too easy, but the only thing that really works. Take a deep breath. Take a step back. Ask yourself what you love about life. Then you will know of what the new foundation can be built.

What most seekers discover over a period of time, is that the self which emerges from the ashes of the past (the ashes of the destruction of your world) is the self who begins to build some manner of new life amongst the ruins of the old. That may sound maudlin, but for me it has been quite the opposite. Once you become a *seer* and realize that the world is comprised of lies and illusions and false beliefs, you begin to realize there really are no rules – you can be, do, and build anything you may desire, and it all begins with a thought.

The reason you experience so much pain and displacement during the *process* of enlightenment is that you are in conflict at some level between what you *believed* about the world and what you are beginning to *see* about the world. Most people – even seekers at the beginning levels – tend to think that it will somehow be different for them. It's natural to want-to-believe that the world around you is real – family, friends, familiar places, comfortable relationships – but the bottom line is that most of those people, places and things are operating under the rules of The Program, and as such they are part of the illusion which begins to crumble as soon as the seeker takes the first step toward letting go of his own false beliefs. That crumbling and dissolution of the consensus can be extremely painful, and is usually the primary reason seekers will turn back to the comfort zone of the matrix.

You ask where you can go after your evolution? You're already there. There is only world, divided infinitely by perception. That being the case – what happens is that you begin to *see* the world differently, even though nothing on the surface has really changed. And as you begin to *see*, you begin to realize that *you* are the creator of reality. You are the god of

147

this brave new world. All acts of creation (or destruction) are ultimately in your hands. What you *do* with that power is always up to you. It isn't that you are isolated. Quite the contrary. You are emerging in to a larger world.

Death Wishes

> *It seems like people who claim they're not suicidal actually do want to die. Maybe they want to be with their deity. Maybe they're just tired of living their boring lives where they feel little passion because passion was a sacrifice they made for the sake of just getting by.*
>
> *The big issue I have with this is not that they have their death wish. The issue is, how do I keep their quasi-suicidal fantasies from pulling me down with them . If I let myself belong and therefore get pulled along by those I'm supposed to trust, I might as well curl up and wait to die, because doing so will wither my soul. If I let it, life will kill me.*

This is where the art of detachment comes into play. The seeker learns to smile and nod at the appropriate pauses in polite conversation, but is no part of the consensual death wish anymore than she is part of the consensual political or religious arena. Some seekers can manage this type of detachment for the sake of maintaining connections with family and friends. Others eventually find it necessary to terminate most of those connections because a definite amount of energy is required to maintain detachment over a long period of time.

The key to maintaining detachment is simple: *Do Not Engage.* It isn't necessary to state your opinion or argue for your own position. It isn't necessary to let others know who you really are. They really don't care. They are too busy maintaining their own agendas to really care about any one else's. One of those ugly truths from the darker teachings. Knowing it can save your sanity – *and* your life.

Ego vs. Empathy
The Selfish Little Self

There's a fine line between empathy and egotism. Having empathy is crucial for seekers, because empathy is nature's mirror – the seeker learns to see herself in others. That isn't to say the seeker is obligated in any way to attempt to save others or even make their lives easier. I help those who cross my path, and those who ask for my help. I don't go looking for causes, but if I do decide to help someone, it is without strings. If I give money to a homeless man, I don't waste time lecturing him. If he wants to buy drugs, that's his choice, and the consequences will be his own. And I don't help him because I feel I *should*. I do it because I can. No other reason. I am occasionally in the position of being able to offer others an alternative or an opportunity. What they do with it is entirely their own affair.

Society is designed to make you feel guilty if you choose not to serve it and worship at the altar of helping others. In reality, this type of paradigm goes back thousands of years – when certain ancient civilizations began to figure out that controlling the masses was largely a matter of placing specific beliefs into the collective unconscious. In reality, everything we do is done for the Self – yes, *every thing*. Anyone who tries to convince you that they are being selfless is either a liar or simply deluded. Even those acts of kindness toward others are really done for the self – to make the self feel better, to make the self believe it is truly helping others. And, indeed, maybe it *is* – but underlying all acts of kindness is an ultimate act of selfishness. And there is nothing wrong with that.

The problem is – people don't take what they *need*. They take all they *can*. They will drain you dry if you let them.

This gets into the programming mechanism of society itself – wherein a series of beliefs are put in place that are intended to control and direct the general population, but a series of beliefs that fall apart whenever someone takes the time and effort to really examine just *what* the belief system is attempting to accomplish. Most times, it's about getting "the little people" to do the bidding of those in positions of power.

Do you think war would exist if the politicians and stuffy world leaders had to lie down in their own droppings in the trenches? But as long as enthusiastic men and women who have been conditioned to believe in "patriotism" can be turned into good little soldiers, war will continue because it ultimately lines the pockets of those same politicians and warmongers who would never think to fight their own battles.

Most people never question the voice of authority because it's just accepted that "this is the way things are." As I've often said to seekers, "You have to *see* beyond the programs before you can *be* beyond them." Most people don't *want* to see beyond the programs, because it generally renders their lives abruptly meaningless and even absurd, so they would rather go on believing the lie than face the consequences of the truth.

Everyone is familiar with the term "loss of faith." Whether in matters of religion or social conditioning, a real loss of faith is devastating, because it rips the foundation out from under you and exposes the bullshit for what it is. Sadly, most people would much rather go right on wading through the crap than making any real effort to clean it up to see what might lie beyond it.

The bottom line is that all those people who are telling you how to live just want you to live as *they* do – because that is what creates and maintains the consensus in the first place. Whenever you stray from the herd, they will begin to exhibit all sorts of bizarre manifestations of Agent Smith – the voice of the matrix attempting to pull you back in line with the lowest common denominator.

Run for your life. And never look back.

There's No Place Like Hell For the Hollydaze

I still get depressed during the holidays. It's like a psychic bombardment of all the insane humans running around looking for more materialistic junk to fill their caves, when none of it matters one wit in the end. That's okay, they can do what they want and even run over one another in the process. Maybe it'll thin the herd a bit.

My problem is getting through the holidays without climbing the clock tower and throwing flaming shit bombs down on all those happy holiday shoppers. I really do find it a burden just to breathe from about November 1 through January 2. No peace to be found. Not even possible to meditate sometimes, the psychic bombardment is so fierce.

I am from a time where there really wasn't a holiday *season* per se. Most families who celebrated Christmas did it in a private manner. Because it is a winter holiday, it was a time when work was uncertain due to weather, and so families would come together in a single household as a means to share resources. The main celebration consisted of good food, conversations around the fire, and the trading of personal inventories (which was much more important before the days of social media and instant gratification).

As for how to avoid the psychic bombardment, the first step is to be aware that the anger and frustration you are feeling are not your own. They are reflections of the phantom humans themselves. What were once traditions of joy have become patterns of competition and expectation. If Betty doesn't get exactly the right gift for Susan, worlds will end and kingdoms shall surely fall. But but but – what if she gets the *right* gift, only to find out that Joan has already gotten it, and for a better price, and wrapped it in more beautiful paper with a bigger bow? Surely *then* the entire world will end and Armageddon will ensue, and fuck Joan all to Hell because she is always for one-upmanship, and now there is no god at all,

151

and that bottle of vicodin is looking better and better, just take the whole damn bunch and be done with this insane life here on this fucked up planet where Joan ruined Christmas!

Perhaps you think I'm being extreme. Think again. This is the mentality many people face. You are simply more *aware* of it during the holidays because the humans engage in the same pointless rituals in greater numbers. And you can rest assured that their combined angers and frustrations are not just harmless emotions. They can become flaming arrows that tend to hit anyone who is psychically open or what some overpaid shrinks like to call "emotionally sensitive." So the choice becomes whether to close oneself off to the madness altogether, join the madmen in their revelry, or find a hole and pull it in after oneself.

Some will surely say that putting up walls or barriers is the way to go, but that generally does not end well for the same reason that wearing masks doesn't end well. Wear the mask long enough, it becomes your new face. Put up the barriers high enough to ward off the lunatics, and you ward off your gnosis as well.

Energy is energy – there is no fundamental difference between good and bad at the level of spirit and particle physics. Simply put, there is no good or evil – only power.

"OMG, didn't Voldemort say the same thing? Is Mikal really Voldemort in disguise?"

Voldemort was a smart guy. Unfortunately, he chose to manifest his power for his own dark agenda. And besides, I made the observation about good, evil and power long before Voldemort was a twinkle in Ms. Rowling's eye. It's one of those dark and nasty truths that's been around since the big bang belched, but one that has been denied for the same amount of time.

People like to believe good and evil are extant entities or forces upon whom they may call for protection, or blame when the dog craps in their shoe. The reality is that it is precisely the same force at work, and that force answers to the name of random chance, filtered through human interpretation in retrospect. Put simply: shit happens.

If a man stops a renowned brain surgeon from stepping in front of a bus, he is considered a hero, written up in the local paper, and may get to shake the mayor's clammy hand at some obscure social function. But if the man he saved is instead a notorious pedophile, the man who saved him might come under some harsh criticism. "Should have let him die!" "Should have thrown him under the bus yourself!" "What were you thinking?"

It makes no difference that the *action* was the same or that the hero had no foreknowledge of the other man's identity. It's how the event is viewed in the aftermath that will inevitably determine whether it is considered good or evil. And either determination is nothing more than a transient conclusion arrived at through the lens of contemporary cultural conditioning and whatever beliefs it may support.

So if you're one who argues for filtering the good from the bad, you might want to take a step back from the precipice of your own conclusions and examine – once again – not only *what* you believe, but *why* you believe it.

When you can find peace amidst the chaos is when you have tapped the hard-wiring between yourself and your Other. The seeker walks through the world and is like a target for the rampant energy that is constantly pouring off of the consensual world. The Other walks through the world *deflecting* that energy because it is not just believed but is *Known* that "This too shall pass." Not just the holiday season, but *all* of it. The worlds are constantly recreating themselves. What is here today is literally gone tomorrow. Knowing this, the Other becomes a reflecting ball, a mirror that does not hold onto any image, but simply allows it to come and go in the breath of a moment.

The best way to escape the madness is to change one's mindset. Reflect rather than absorb.

Even seekers become most conflicted during the traditional holiday season – torn between wanting to be with family (or at least their lingering illusion of family), and a new level of awareness that makes it impossible not to see the absolute folly in it all.

I hope this season will bring you happiness and a few smiles. I have found it to be an excellent opportunity for observing just how un-real "reality" really is.

> *In centuries too distant to imagine*
> *I will bring you improbable gifts,*
> *things that cannot exist:*
> > *snowmen crafted of Martian ice,*
> > *a cat that can never die,*
> > *a bubble containing a siren's cry*
> > *the rusted corpse of Time.*
>
> *This is the vampire's Christmas...*
> *found in the darkest regions*
> *of little girl lost boy dreams.*

Bible Thumping

I just realized the Bible and other sacred texts sound idiotic if you consider they are written from the point of view of a commanding God – all those prohibitions, laws, boundaries. Yet the same text could be read as the voice of the Other, and the result is uncanny. Then it reads like that secret voice that guides you to do the necessary. And if you don't – well, then the wages of sin are indeed death.

I do believe it is an older instruction, aimed at an older generation of Mankind, an older breed of mystics. I believe it would be silly to follow it to the letter. Yet it is understandable why people would take it so seriously. I could imagine receiving a revelation so compelling that I take it beyond the personal, put it out as universal law. But I realize all revelations are temporary, intimate – a holy book written anew at every moment.

Excellent observations. I've always felt that the Bible and other holy texts have a deep truth within them – the problem is that those who follow the organized religion have warped the words to suit their own agendas, and so whatever deeper meaning may exist is lost except to those few who actually *see* what you have just expressed.

It has also been speculated that early Christianity was a mushroom cult – wherein those who had journeyed with the ally took it upon themselves to attempt to express what they had *seen* in their mystical travels. As anyone who has experienced the mushroom knows, attempting to translate that kind of transcendental experience into transient language is altogether impossible.

One reason I give some credence to the idea of a mushroom cult is that one of the most important aspects of God is the use of the phrase "I Am." In the book of Exodus, God says to Moses, *"I am that I am. Thus shalt thou say unto the children of Israel, I Am hath sent me unto you."*

This is allegedly when Moses was talking to a burning bush. As anyone who has experienced the psilocybin mushroom also knows, objects may appear so bright as to burn one's eyes, so it stands to reason that someone in that time period might have thought the bush was actually on fire. In reality (whatever that may be), the mushroom causes the optical system to become hyper-sensitive. One can perceive the physical distance between the stars because visual acuity is so greatly enhanced.

In my own writings, I have used the term *I-Am* to indicate that I exist not only in space and time, but beyond all idea of time, and outside of physical space. To say *I-Am* is to say one is eternal, transcendental, ascended from human form to something other-than-human. The recognition of this state of being within oneself often comes during a journey with the mushroom ally, so there may indeed be some dark credence to the notion that God is an immortal spore spawned in some alien sea and sent to earth on the solar winds of the timeless voyage of the Forever Young.

The Energy Body and Modern Medicine

The energy body can't really be harmed except in the most extreme circumstances. What *can* be harmed is the connection and communication between the heavy body (organic body) and the energy body (inorganic body).

Modern medicine tends to treat symptoms far more than it targets the actual source of an ailment, so the result is that many of the medicines being prescribed aren't really cures, but instead palliative measures at best. They can't harm the energy body, but they can certainly damage the organic body, which is why most commercials that contain the words "Ask your doctor" now come with a lengthy list of side effects that would make even a vampire cringe. Your foot may fall off and you may die in a writhing mass of gelatinous goo, but your toenails will look great in your coffin!

New agers who like to say medicine can harm the energy body really don't know their earlobe from their persqueeter. So I want to stress that energy is energy. It isn't affected by what you may do to your body, but if the damage to the organic body is severe enough, the energy body can become distanced or even severed from the organic body over a period of time. This is what happens in cases of extreme drug overdose or what has been referred to as "induced schizophrenia."

When the energy body and the physical body become separated from one another through some form of trauma (whether accidental or intentional) the chi falls out of balance and the organic body falters, like a car without a driver. The energy body continues on its journey until such time as the organic body dies or heals, but the communication between the two is lost – sometimes temporarily, sometimes permanently.

There are several institutions whose sole purpose is to maintain the status quo of the matrix.

1. Religion
2. Politics
3. The medical profession

I'm sure there are lots of others, but these are the three major ones I have observed over a very long period of time. When humans can be assimilated by any or all of these institutions, their chances for evolution drop exponentially.

Evolution, Revolution and De-evolution

Some might say "It's not my problem!" but is that a true statement? I'm not so sure. It <u>becomes</u> my at a very fundamental level when the dominant belief systems threaten an evolving species. It's why people like Mikal do what they do – subverting the dominant paradigm – and it's why some of us will take on that same task as time goes by.

To use the vampire example, some of us will become "creators" while others might not. Some of us will be world changers and paradigm crashers while others will settle into a solitary corner of personal immortality. But those who willfully return to the program will be nothing more than food for worms. I see too many wannabe seekers on the Immortal Spirit forum who dabble in the shallow end for awhile, then as soon as their beliefs are challenged – even in the most minor and polite manner – they pitch a butt-hurt bitch and run screaming back to their comfort zones. Maybe to be expected. Can't bake a cake without breaking some egos.

If you want to live in a world where immortality is possible, you have to create that world before you can inhabit it. This is a much simplified statement which should not be taken at face value, but studied and observed from a real life platform for a very long time before it can be wholly *seen* for the truth it is.

I am not the least bit certain it is something that can even be vaguely understood by most humans, or even by most seekers. Reason being – most really can't see the forest for the trees. It might best be boiled down to this: Everything begins with a thought. Followed immediately by: Every thought must be forced to go thru the motions of actually occurring if it is to have manifestation.

> *The Wright Brothers didn't just dream of flying.*
> *They built a plane. And only <u>then</u> could they bring their*
> *dream into being.*

What must be understood is that individuals have always held the power to evolve *as* individuals, to attain the immortal condition. But the consensual paradigm is such that humans are not only born mortal and transient, they are conditioned to *remain* mortal and transient, and stupidity begets stupidity, and so it goes round and round again and again.

It only requires a small amount of observation to realize that women had virtually no rights up until a few short years ago. Minorities were considered inferior by virtue of skin color or race. The list is long.

Things change only when *you* change them – and that includes the false beliefs which are rampant in today's world and have resulted in the sad state of affairs one might observe on the nightly news, in the streets, or right next door.

Am I saying that immortality should be available to everybody? It already *is* – but they will *still* have to go thru the process of actually evolving, and most simply won't. So what will eventually happen is another divided consensus such as what occurred when some of the great apes made the decision to evolve and others went back to the trees. The species will split, as it has done countless times throughout history, as it does on a daily basis when you stop to think that your own evolution and individuation is entirely a *choice*.

You are choosing to evolve – but make no mistake: those who are choosing to remain in the trees are a very real threat, in the sense that they are the storm troopers who will try to drag you back into the program, and they are the True Believers who will put a bullet through your head (or a stake in your heart) in the name of their god. Why? Because you threaten their comfortable status quo.

It really is that simple. And that sad.

Fate, Destiny and Predestination

I'm enraged by the concept of destiny or fate. This belief gives you no choice on the events that may happen or will happen to your life.

Ultimately, there are only two ways to look at the idea of predestination.

1. We are all victims of predestination.

2. Predestination doesn't exist, but is circumvented by free will.

If you choose door #1, then there is essentially no hope.

If you choose door #2, then destiny and fate become probability waves rather than certainties. Meaning – even if it is *likely* that something will unfold in a particular way, you can choose to believe that you have the free will to alter its course – and ultimately it cannot be otherwise. You might *conclude* that you were therefore predestined to change this or that, but that really isn't the case in a quantum universe.

The only way destiny or fate play out is if you are passive and allow things to take the course of least resistance. If left to its own devices, water will seek its own course based on gravity and obstacles. But you can change the course of an entire river by rechanneling the water (energy) through the use of your own choices. A dam here. A tunnel there.

You are the most powerful being in the universe. Fate and destiny should tremble.

Beings Who Are Going to Die?

What is death? Is it really an inevitable occurrence? Where do we really stand with regard to our bid for freedom?

Humans die not because they must, but because that is the nature of their communal belief. It is the dictate of the consensus, and so the program has become a biological imperative even though biology itself is only an illusory manifestation of energy, and is not truly organic at all if one is willing to *see* beyond the veil and peer deep into the scheme of the dream. To think of oneself as a biological entity is to enter the battle already defeated, no?

You ask about death as if it is a reality, and so you are accepting already some measure of your programming, and it is sufficient to kill you because you already believe you are a being who is going to die.

Does it trouble you that I might challenge one of the very cornerstones of the human belief system? *Are* you a being who is going to die? Are you a *being* at all, or is that, too, only a mode of perception from which you then attach meaning and define absolutes? And in defining absolutes (you are a being who is going to die, you say), do you then predetermine through the perception that you are *alive*, that life must naturally have its opposite (death), and so you enter into the arena of the living already predetermined to be a being who is going to stop being?

The secret to living forever is Knowing you were never alive to begin with, because even the word 'alive' carries with it the baggage of centuries, the belief systems of an entire species. To believe (an assumption) that you are alive (a concept, but an erroneous one) is to step into the battlefield not as a warrior but as a victim of the consensus.

What to do? Are you willing to have one more world yanked out from under you? Are you able to consider that everything you believe about death and life are only comfort zones intrinsic to the mindset of your ancestors, and so you carry them with you as cancers on your Dream even when you may think you have dispensed with them?

The secret to immortality is this: when you know you are already dead, you may transcend this prison that insists you are a being who is going to die. The immortals do not *believe* they will live forever. Neither do they Know it. It is simply their nature to do so because the foundation of their knowing is based on the *I-Am* rather than the weight of any consensus.

> *We cast no reflection because we are whole unto ourselves, and so what might be seen in the mirror is only what humans choose to project. Yet it is an image projected on a transparent screen, and cannot reflect – for to reflect would be to enter again into the agreement, yes?*

We thrive on existence itself, taking sustenance from the pulsing heart of the sentient universe, knowing it is an endless river and can never be drained, for it stems from the self, and therefore can never die.

To live forever is to undo death, to be as legends speak of, undead – but also un-alive, yet in being un-alive we finally Will ourselves to Unconditional *Life*. To be immortal is to have no opposite, for it is in the friction of opposition that deterioration begins.

Perhaps it may best understood like this: *"Until you have grasped this: 'die and be transformed!' you will be nothing but a somber guest on the sorry earth*[23]*."*

Examine those words from beyond the words and listen with your heart for what they mean. It is more than any casual thesis I am asking you to write. Instead, it is the rewriting of your entire paradigm that will set you free, but only when you *see* the Dream from beyond even the lucidity of the Dream.

---

[23] Johann Wolfgang von Goethe

The Ascended Masters

I found myself reading your book in the beginning, years ago. I was looking into vampires because of energy transfer and withdrawal. I wonder if you are the big kahuna and a shaman, but at the same time I wonder if you are luring all of us crazies in to exploitation. If that's the case, why?

I did not become who and what *I-Am* by accident, nor without guidance. I could say it is my obligation to give back in direct proportion to what I have received, but that would be a lie. Why do I do this? For myself. I am a selfish bastard and the dark truth is that I gain Knowledge through the processes at work in my sustained interaction with seekers. Seekers ask questions that are difficult if not impossible to answer, and in doing so they force me to delve ever deeper into the endless rabbit hole of perception and assimilation.

Evolution of consciousness is a bootstrap process, and you will not succeed by reading alone. To attain the immortal condition, one must not only remove the existing programs, but replace them with Knowledge that extends far beyond what is presently understood or believed. One way to do this is to be always testing and expanding your Knowledge through gnosis. Gnosis is forced into action when conversations exceed the sum of present information, and the seeker is compelled to look within, where all answers reside.

What I do here is not any noble venture. It is part of the work, and it is a work that is eternal. Attaining the immortal condition is the first step. *Maintaining* it is the next. I am beyond the ability of death to undo, not by default, but by choice, by action, and by force of will. *That* is why I do it.

Why help a bunch of lost seekers who want to know the answers to everything? Why come off like you have the answers but make it a huge riddle? Why not just give it all to us straight – the truth.

I have. Many times. If you still don't *see* it, you may be looking with the eyes of expectation rather than the eyes of observation. *Teachings of the Immortals* contains many truths. The information on the immortalis-animus.com website contains many more. The Immortal Spirit forum is filled with truth. Are you asking the right questions? And if you are, have you mastered the difficult art of assimilating the answers?

> *Isis was supposed to be an ascended master. I believe that the ascended masters can in fact help you progress, but it's more of a spiritual path than becoming physically immortal.*

Becoming immortal is a spiritual path in the sense that it is a shifting and realignment of Spirit that enables the seeker to shed the programs which bind her to mortality.

How do you define "ascended masters?" Do you know any? I am pushing you on this not to be an obnoxious bastard, but because so much of what humans believe is based on what they have been *told* to believe, and not on what they have experienced directly.

Some of the most difficult programs to unravel are those centered around religion and spirituality. Most new age beliefs are simply that: beliefs. Others are extrapolations which are vastly inaccurate – they might have good intentions, but it's rather like standing in a garbage dump and declaring, "Look at all the garbage these flies have created!" What may *appear* to be reasonable often *isn't*.

Ultimately, the only ascended master who can help you is your Other. You might gather information from other sources, but actual Knowledge will come only from your own interactions with the infinite.

Spirit

What, in your eyes, is the spirit, Mikal? And what is the assemblage point?

There is no easy way to define Spirit. It is the fluttering of awe in the center of the chest. It is the longing in the heart that causes you to wonder and to wander in search of that which cannot be named. It is the essence of All life – not just human life, but *all* life. It is the cohesion of the self that is the crossroads between self and Other, mortal and immortal. Spirit is the spark of creation from which all life springs. It is not sentient in and of itself, but is the vessel of All sentience. It is what some have called "the force."

The assemblage point is every bit as difficult to define, yet it is simply the lens through which you experience the world. If you view it as a camera through which you are looking, it becomes possible to imagine that the lens can get stuck in one position if left there too long.

With that in mind, the normal position of the assemblage point focuses on what you might call ordinary life. One becomes programmed to the normal world and as a result one tends to only experience that world unless something sufficiently unusual comes along to shift the assemblage point to a different location. Trauma (physical or emotional) can cause such a shift. Loss of a loved one. An unexpected encounter with the unknown (getting abducted by aliens tends to shift the AP profoundly). Intense danger. There are many factors that can shift the AP instantly and dramatically.

I ask about the assemblage point because I related "shifting the assemblage point" to "a shifting of spirit." I have also had the thought that making the shift to immortality is just making a shift in the assemblage point.

In some ways, that is true. It is the assemblage point that holds one's programs intact, and when those programs are eliminated, the assemblage point is able to move to a position that is outside the box of humanform thinking and conditioning. When that occurs, one then has the opportunity to move the AP to the position where immortality is no longer considered an impossibility. From there, the step to transmogrification becomes far more accessible.

You might also consider the assemblage point to be a mindset through which one's identity is created and maintained. However, I would classify that statement as truth primarily for phantoms – those who are *in* the world, *of* the world, and content with their comfort zones and programs. You've heard the term "He's just set in his ways"? That would indicate a fixed position of the assemblage point.

Food for thought: Death is a position of the assemblage point.

Death is a Position of the Assemblage Point

You said, "Death is a position of the assemblage point. If one is dead, who or what would be assembling "death"? You have my curiosity tweaked!

This is where the road twists and bends and up becomes down and down becomes a spiral which is really a worm hole in the apple of forbidden knowledge.

Death is a position of the assemblage point. And it is also proof that you are not your body. There is the mortal self, through which the assemblage point projects what you believe to be reality. And there is the Other, who exists outside the box and beyond the ability of death to undo. It could be observed in most ordinary humans that death occurs when the assemblage point moves to a position that is without reference points within the world of matter and men. There is

166

the perception of nothing, yet that very nothing is a perception, which implies there is something doing the perceiving.

In most ordinary humans, the Other is not sufficiently cohesive to withstand the ravages of eternity, and so consciousness and awareness dissipate rapidly, to be reabsorbed into the fabric of the multiverse as their component parts – simple energy, without identity or cohesion. For the seeker who has a sufficiently cohesive twin, the same awareness moves into the energetic vessel of the twin, where it is rekindled and integrated into what the Toltecs call "the totality of oneself." At that point, a certain duality is achieved, wherein one is both dead and alive simultaneously, or, if you prefer "undead."

Clearly this is simplified look at a vastly complex subject, but if you look at it from the corner of the third eye, you will *see* why the immortals say "Death is a position of the assemblage point."

What's crucial to remember is that it is a position that can (and must) be shifted from organic to inorganic, in the blink of an eye.

From Organic to Inorganic
The winter holiday is known as Asylum,
not for any reason,
but because that's how it's always been.
Carols are sung by hallucinations posing as children
and the Mayor of Mourning rings thirteen bells
at the mid of night on Asylum's Eve.

If a raven comes to your window calling
with sprig of poison holly,
you'll know that you've been chosen
to live forever in Umbernight,
now and forever existing
at the fingertips of your magick.

The Dream Body

You taught in your book that the Other is the dream body. I read in another book that a person who has attained the ability to see will realize that when people have sex with each other, the other person is not another person, but everyone has sex only with his own dream body. Does this mean that when I make love with a girl, the truth is that I only have sex with my own Other, but due to the overlay I fail to perceive this? Is this correct or nonsense?

Whether it's correct or nonsense depends on what perspective one is choosing to employ. From a strictly dayshine perspective, where all the rules of The Program are in effect, it is pure nonsense – because the woman with whom you are making love is a being unto herself, extant and individual. From a more quantum perspective, it could be *seen* that all things are connected at the level of energy, and so (to employ a new age feel-goodism), "We are all one."

Personally, I don't care for the "We are all one" philosophy because it implies that there is no individuation. And to an immortal, individuation is what separates the immortal identity from the mortal coil.

With that said, I'm going to be practical for a moment and say that when you engage with the Other, you are making love. When you engage with just a mortal human, you are having sex, or simply fucking. Nothing wrong with that. But in my opinion, having sex with your Other is life-altering, and potentially fatal in the sense that the desire to conjoin in *all* ways kicks in, and when it does there is no going back to your humanform life. Yes, it is that serious. And it is why don Juan issued the warning...

"The sorcerer who comes face to face with his double
is a dead sorcerer."

–Carlos Castaneda

It can be helpful to think of the mortal self and immortal other as matter and antimatter. If they meet under the wrong circumstances, it could be potentially fatal to the mortal self in the sense that the compulsion to (re)conjoin would be so intense that the human body could not survive. Those who have encountered their Other in dreaming or astral can attest to this. Anyone who has actually met their twin "in the flesh" (through skinwalking or otherwise) can tell you that they were lucky to survive the experience at all.

> *The natural compulsion between mortal self and immortal Other is to conjoin – to become one, to embrace the totality which is greater than the sum of its parts. When that occurs, one either transcends, transmogrifies, or drops dead, depending on the extent to which the seeker has evolved at the moment this meeting occurs.*

The danger is very real, and also very seductive *because* of that very danger.

This is the way of the dark evolution.

Ego and the Higher Self

I've heard the words "ego" and "higher self" being thrown around and I've wondered what exactly is meant by them. When you start looking up meditation, spirituality, and things of that nature you're sure to find someone talking about letting go of the ego. So the ego is, from what I understand, a person's sense of self. Is the ego part of and/or sustained by the internal dialog? And, if the internal dialog were to be silenced, would the ego vanish as well?

It depends on what century one is from. The word "ego" has gotten a bad name with the arrival of the new age bandwagon, but without the ego, *you* would not exist as anything other than a blob of non-cohesive consciousness hanging in space somewhere in the vicinity of Uranus.

From the perspective of a seeker, it might be best understood to say that the ego is the mortal self and the higher self is the immortal Other. That's the much-simplified explanation, though there are countless shades of grey in between. Some will argue that the ego is the personality and that it must be shed and lost and crucified at all costs on a holy wooden cross, but those who say such things are usually those with something to sell, and in fact it is their own ego that pushes them to tell you the ego is your worst enemy when, in fact, it is *their* best friend. Ah well... such is the dance of the devil who does not exist in and of himself, but is created from moment to moment by those who say they seek to warn you away from him, but who are really singing him into being through their own actions.

To be fair (nothing in life is fair), it could be noted that what some new age mumbo jumblers refer to as the ego might be *seen* by sufficiently advanced seekers as the self that has been created and maintained by The Program. At that level of thinking, the ego is the phantom self – the practitioner and protector of The Status Quo, the believer in the false beliefs foisted upon him by the Program itself. At that level, *if* that is what is meant by ego, then, yes, that is the self which must be destroyed. Unfortunately, most so-called teachers stop there and fail to mention that it is necessary to replace those false beliefs with a foundation of self-realized truths, lest the seeker fall splat-first into the abyss and emerge as the very zombie foretold in legends (or at least in *The Walking Dead*).

> *And then you have what some people call the higher self. Wikipedia says it is "a term associated with multiple belief systems but its basic premise describes an eternal, omnipotent, conscious, and intelligent being, who is one's real self". Sounds like what the Other is supposed to be. Except every time I hear about it from someone (usually a*

YouTube vid) they don't talk about creating it or falling in love with it at all. Just connecting with it. Which doesn't make any sense to me at all.

This is because most jabber-babblers on YouTube are part of The Program's mouthpiece, even though they may believe themselves to be enlightened messengers from the Andromeda Galaxy. They are caught in the leg trap of cultural religiosity whether they realize it or not – a belief system that creates a sense of entitlement in its victims by making them believe their "soul" is an automatic gift handed out at birth along with toes and genitals, when the reality is that the soul is like anything else. It must be fed and nurtured if it is ever to grow into anything more than a distant spark.

The soul is nothing more than the instinct to bring the Other into being – for without it there is always a sense of emptiness, distance, loneliness, grief. It is only when the mortal self begins to reach out and project beyond himself that he begins to literally create the only thing that will slowly begin to fill those chasms in his soul.

As this occurs, and as the seeker instructs, "Make me whole," the Other begins to take on a life-energy (animus) of its own, and goes out into the world (which has no limitations to the twin – past, present, future) and amasses experiences which some mistakenly refer to as past lives but which are more accurately quantum manifestations and movements of the energy structure which is the twin.

The reason you must fall in love with it (whether romantically or only at a platonic level of friendship if you're squeamish) is because – as I have said many times – love is the reason. The human animal is driven by love in all things, at one level or another. There are those who have argued vehemently with me on this subject, but if you follow the energetic strands which bind all things together, you will *see* that even the things humans may do because they have to are done out of love for something or someone, or simply out of a love of life and the need to survive.

You may not go to work because you love your job, but because you love life, and so you work in a consensus gone mad because it is the only way (at least you believe it is) to keep the roof over your head and the cat well-supplied with catnip. If you have not yet read *Teachings of the Immortals*, this is a subject that repeats frequently. Love is the reason. It is the *only* reason.

In actuality, there are no shades of grey between the ego and the higher self. The ego is "mortal." The higher self is "immortal." Knowing one from the other is what will save your life. The rest is just window dressing and semantics. Sure, the ego can be healthy, but it can also be a phantom that has convinced you it is healthy.

What Does One *Do* With Immortality?

Immortality provides a long calendar for accomplishing things, but also the simultaneous understanding that most things make no difference in the big picture. So if one chooses to cure cancer or train cattle to dance, it is as an act of controlled folly.

Immortality is not a linear-time prospect, so it's not a matter of filling one's days with activities. That's the human mindset. The immortal mindset (and ability set) is such that one is not confined to a linear experience of life, death, the universe, and everything in between. "Yesterday" I spent a lifetime or two in Key West long before the coming of the European scourge. I did a lot of reading on my Kindle while there, because the Kindle exists in the hologram even though it did not exist within the sphere of time where I found myself. Such is the paradox of immortal perception.

All who embark on this path are engaged in what Crowley called "The Great Work" - the work of a lifetime (or more). I'm not referring to reincarnation, but to moving in and out of the hologram through the wormholes of time. Today it may seem you are trapped in the internal dialog of the consensus, but yesterday and tomorrow you will be walking the dark nightroads of London with (or *as*) your Other in the sideways manifestations of eternity. You may call it a dream, an astral journey, or a vision, but what is Real is Real, no matter how it enters your conscious experience. This is the work of The Work. It is a living poem with some verses being haiku and others dull sonnets.

Most of all, immortality provides options and opportunities - for those who choose to dabble in the ongoing affairs of the mortal world, that is.

If there is a downside, it is knowing that everything around you will change, and quite likely, die.

Everything has its price, including immortality.

What is the Nature of Attraction?

I don't really enjoy interacting with humans but I like to know that they are within relative proximity of self. Does consciousness just naturally gravitate to other consciousness, or is this attraction actually rooted in part of the program, or something else entirely?

I am not a particularly social animal. Humans tend to be tedious for the most part, with serious seekers being the only real exception. And comedians.

Does consciousness gravitate to other consciousness? There are conflicting ideas on this. In my opinion, there are two primary categories.

1. "Conglomerate consciousness" – wherein humans tend to gravitate into communities, not only for purposes of survival, but for a sense of companionship and camaraderie.

2. Individuated consciousness – wherein one is essentially a loner, self-sufficient and independent, often to a fault.

What's interesting is that these types of awareness may also extend beyond the threshold of death, assuming the individuals have amassed sufficient cohesion to make such a transition. There are those who more or less flock together within the "All" after death. And there are those who demand their individuated *I-Am* and walk alone.

How does this relate to the idea of old souls and new souls?

There might be certain exceptions (such as a seeker who has a highly developed Other that has lived multiple lifetimes), but for the most part, I have found that people believe in old/new souls in the same way they might believe in angels and demons. They are common beliefs, but that doesn't make them true.

A lot of new agers also like to use the idea of old and new souls to create a paradigm of superiority. I once attended a new age conference on a lark and found all the twitter and twatter to be little more than a resurrection of the old game of King of the Mountain. "I'm a very old soul," one of the speakers said to begin her lengthy diatribe. "I've been in incarnation since long before the pharaohs."

Of course, her reign as King of the Mountain was short-lived when someone in the audience – wearing a colorful caftan and enough crystals to power a fleet of starships – said with great enthusiasm, "Me, too! I was there when the great darkness came to wipe out the sun for a million years!"

The speaker maintained her pretense of calm, but it was easy to *see* her seething just beneath that amethyst healing pendant dangling from her pulsating throat somewhere in the vicinity of the fifth chakra.

It's all made up, of course. Any doubt of this, please don't take my word for it, but access your own inner bullshit detector through gnosis.

Old souls and new souls are nothing more than illusions within the illusion. Never forget – Time is the first fundamental lie. Without it, there is only awareness, and the depth to which it has been honed through the interface between the mortal self and infinite Other. And, yes, I'm quite sure even *that* will sound like new age woo-woo to some. And yet, to those who have experienced it, no explanation is necessary. To those who haven't, no explanation is possible.

Time is a river
from which immortals
do not drink.

The Body

I have maintained a belief that only I can heal myself. Many years ago I had a vision and was shown that all healing therapies are just part of the matrix. I get that. I also understand (as per your words of advice) that truly falling in love with the twin can be life-changing and have a remarkable healing effect on the organic body. I know common sense is called for, but I have been on the healing merry-go-round for so long that have lost my way a bit. How do you navigate it all?

You're treading close to a dangerous truth when you say, "*All* healing therapies on this planet are just part of the matrix." So many people think that immortality (or even good health) is a matter of what you eat and how you manage the body. While that might (or might not) be marginally true on a purely organic level, the reality is that no matter *what* you eat or do not eat, no matter what you drink or do not drink, none of that will make you immortal. And to be dangerously honest, it won't even do much for maintaining the body or healing it. The real trick is what you *believe* about what you eat, drink, or consume as supplements.

The darker teaching comes into play when one realizes that the price for awareness is the sacrifice of that same belief. Once you are truly a seer, what is *seen* is what you have already said – it's all part of the matrix. From that perspective, it is then rather difficult to have a fervent and pious faith in food or pharmaceuticals. This is when Belief has become, simply, "belief." And therein lies the irony.

The seeker's goal is to demolish all programs, but in doing so it also begins to seem one has shut down the very beliefs that work toward maintaining the organic form. What to do?

What I am going to say here is intended primarily for those who have been on the path for awhile and who already know the truth behind it. This is not something one should take to heart if one is still ensconced in the matrix and adheres to the common beliefs about what health means and how it may be achieved.

The body is a flawed organic construct, but it is made of energy at its core (as all things are). This presents a duality and a dichotomy from the start. The energy itself is flawless and eternal. The organic construct which is being maintained by that energy is, on the other hand, subject to deterioration and decay. Taken from a purely *organic* perspective, one is fighting a losing battle. Taken from a purely *energetic* perspective, not one bit of it makes one bit of bitty difference.

"Eh? What is Mikal saying?"

Simply this: for the sorcerer who has shed his organic programming it can be observed that what one eats or drinks really has no direct bearing on the sorcerer's physical (organic) body. I have known advanced seekers (sorcerers, if you prefer) who eat a steady diet of Taco Bell and consume enough alcohol to float the *Titanic*, and they remain in a good state of health despite whatever health conditions they have been told to believe they are carrying with them.

What does this mean? Essentially, you are not what you eat. *You are what you Know.* Even if the organic body has health issues (I'm referring primarily to so-called diseases or chronic conditions), it is possible to experience an almost perfect state of well-being, not as a result of what one does or doesn't do on an organic level, but as a result of what one *is* at the core level of flawless energy.

This is another way in which the seeker consumes animus – not by imbibing naked juice but by literally projecting, flowing, and *being* in the state of awareness that not only tells you that you are a being of energy, but proves it to you by allowing you to reach a state of being wherein you are calling upon the energetic nature of your being to maintain the body, rather than trying to *convince* the body it is made of energy.

Again, I must stress that I am not encouraging anyone to take up a diet of cheese pretzels and rum. But to the sorcerer who *sees*, there is no difference between that cheese pretzel and a rutabaga. This is one of the darker teachings because it violates everything humans are taught to believe. For those who are still thinking inside the matrix, it is necessary to continue to make choices according to what you truly *believe* at the time. If you believe supplements and salads are the key to happiness, then that may well be your experience. But there are realities which extend far beyond those limited beliefs and self-perpetuating experiences.

As you read this, be aware of your intrinsic reactions. This will give you a better idea of where you are within (or outside of) the dominant paradigm.

The Quantum Multiverse

Ultimately, the "universe" (aka multiverse) is indeed finite, but only in the sense of time (the first fundamental lie). As the universe breathes in and breathes out (the big bang and the big collapse) the *only* thing constant and unchanging is the energy itself. All matter and antimatter rise and fall (creation and obliteration) but the subatomic particles of which they are comprised never change – they can neither be created or destroyed, so in a sense, they exist apart from the hologram. In another sense, it *is* the hologram's component structure.

As for immortals? Immortals are beings of energy, or beings of light, if you prefer – ironic though that may be to those who identify with the vampire paradigm. As a result, the component energy that makes an immortal is infused with consciousness, which can only change form, but may never be created or destroyed.

In the same sense, the immortal awareness exists outside of the first fundamental lie, so the rise and fall of space and time are altogether irrelevant.

Talking Yourself Out of Immortality

Anyone has the opportunity to talk themselves out of anything by trying to prove or disprove the teachings. One seeker may use his knowledge of quantum science to talk himself out of immortality, and it would not distress me in the least. If others choose to follow him, that is their choice and that would also have no effect on my emotional well-being. Harsh as this may seem, I have no investment in whether anyone succeeds or fails in their journey toward immortality. I have only what I consider to be a personal obligation to make certain information available. What anyone does with it is entirely up to them.

From time to time, someone seems to have a great need to disprove the teachings with science, rather than using personal experience to validate the teachings for themselves. I will not attempt to defend the teachings by getting into extended scientific discussions, for the simple reason that science (*all* science) is just one more religion in the sense that it depends on hypotheses and theories – which are nothing more than a re-naming of faith and belief.

The teachings are meant to move the seeker *beyond* the need for the comfort zones which will ultimately prevent that seeker from ever truly understanding them at the core level. Any leap in spiritual awakening and evolution only occurs when the seeker is willing to let go of the things that are preventing him from making that very leap. Some can let go. Others never do. The results speak for themselves.

Does this mean one needs to abandon common sense? No. It simply means that there is a mindset for the world of matter and men. And there is an entirely different mindset for the infinite. Only when the seeker sufficiently embraces the concept of co-existent duality does it become possible to have it both ways.

Really, though, it's all about surrender to the Other. The seeker who fails to surrender will always be at war.

Anyone can ask me questions which I will not be able to answer with what they would consider to be 'scientific accuracy,' and that is the world of logic. But as I've stated many times, a seeker can easily understand logic through the eyes of magic, but will never understand magic through the eyes of logic. Either someone enters a quest for immortality based on a spiritual yearning or calling (which defies all scientific explanation) or one stands outside the journey and attempts to analyze it to death in what is really an attempt to shore up their own faltering belief systems.

It is said that fear is the first enemy of a seeker, and there is no greater fear than having one's world dismantled and eventually destroyed. In particular, very young seekers often still believe the world is held together by quantifiable things that can be proven with a slide rule or microscope. The reality, of course, is that it is only belief that is holding the world together. When that belief is released is when one enters into what mystics have called "a separate reality."

Only from that position of the assemblage point does the journey truly begin.

Keeping Light On the Mirror

I recently had a sweet reminder from my twin when I peeked into Teachings of the Immortals at random and came across the section "Keeping Light on the Mirror." As I read it, I got the impression that the twin was saying, "Don't forget about me," and also, "My energy comes from you; if you don't give me energy, I cannot give you energy." I feel like there is a lot more, but I can't quite grasp it, particularly the first sentence about Eternity trembling before the vampire king. Could you elaborate?

It seems appropriate to post the entry in full.

(Excerpt from *Teachings of the Immortals*)

Eternity crosses herself like a virgin on her wedding night, trembling before the vampire king in his rumpled tux. Does this mirror still reflect or has it gone dark? There is not a moment I do not think of you, yet time passes in silence and I say nothing because there are no quandaries, no conundrums. I appease myself with old books and well-read scraps of poetry, longing for a new infusion of energy, aching to give it to you, knowing instead it is something only you can do.

So, when you ask, "Does the mirror still reflect or has it gone dark?" who is the mirror and who is the reflection? In my mind, when I ask who is the observer and who is the observed, it is like a Zen koan, attempting to pop myself out of everyday thinking and into a looking-glass world where I am both the reflected observing and the observer reflected.

The mirror is both – the mortal self and the immortal Other. For practical purposes, the self is both observer and observed. From a more metamystical perspective, the mortal self is the source (at least in the beginning, if any beginning, middle or end can be found), and the immortal Other is the reflection. One is solid and organic, while the other is energy that takes on form as the light on the mirror becomes more intense through practice and relentless Intent.

If the mortal source begins to grow dull, so does the reflection. It isn't that the Other won't reflect and provide energy to the mortal self. It is that the Other *can't* when the mortal self is no longer projecting the energetic reflection.

As a bit of clarification, that particular entry was written to an apprentice who had gone a considerable distance down the path, then inevitably lost interest and turned her attentions to typical humanform distractions. She had the idea that once the Other was generated, no other maintenance was required. She now wanders the banks of Lethe, always hungry for something she cannot quite remember and will probably never be able to touch again.

This is the danger of apathy and the spoils of believing one is *There* when one is still (and always) on The Way. People lose interest because The Way is not always easy, especially for someone who is in love with their comfort zones. This person allowed herself to be lured back into phantomhood because she *enjoys* being a phantom. It really is that simple.

The "light on the mirror" entry in *Teachings of the Immortals* is a reminder and a warning – a message from the Other that if the source goes dark, the reflection may disappear from the mirror altogether – shedding more light on the old notion that "vampires cast no reflection."

Everything is a choice and all choices are equal. The consequences aren't always equal, but that is *also* a choice.

Being aware at all times is something that comes with practice and (the illusion of) time. As one *becomes* the way instead of struggling to be *on* the way, this becomes automatic. It may still be tiring at times because the mortal world lures one into comfortable numbness, but eventually awareness really does become the new normal.

The Immortal Archetype

Can you give us an example of a true vampire archetype/lifestyle? It's hard to envision my double as a vampire when you destroyed my idea of what a vampire is.

Your twin must be what *you* need and perceive it to be. I have used the word vampire because the traditional archetype of a vampire is an immortal who...

1. Walks a solitary path outside of time. (Understanding "outside of time" is an assignment unto itself).

2. A vampire is a being who was once mortal, but who has transformed, transcended or transmogrified as a matter of his own intent and will.

3. In traditional lore, vampires can bi-locate (be in two places at once). This is an oblique reference to the mortal self and immortal twin, much warped over the centuries until now it is nothing but an obscure and seemingly occult trait assigned to the traditional view of a vampire. The reality is that you *are* in two (or more) places at once, through the quantum entanglement with the Other.

4. A vampire is an energy being – the inorganic Other as contrasted to the organic mortal self. Because the vampire is made of energy, it adheres to the law which states, "Energy cannot be created or destroyed, it can only change form." Therefore the vampire may appear as anything it chooses, so long as it possesses the personal power to do so. Many maintain the same form indefinitely. Others may seem like

shape-shifters. Still others have no discernible form whatsoever (yet they are just as viable as any other manifestation).

5. A vampire possesses the power to "turn" others, but not in the sense you may think. In short, I can turn you but only through knowledge and the extension of your own personal power. No one can make you immortal but yourself.

6. A vampire thrives on animus – the living *force* of Life. It is not necessary to take this essence from others (bloodletting is just a myth, and a dangerous one). The force of Life surrounds us at all times and is there for the taking. Not by taking life, but by ingesting the energetic animus itself, directly." (*"Mikal keeps repeating that! Does he think we're really hung up on the idea of drinking blood?"*) Yes, Mikal *knows* many who follow this path are hung up on that notion - but that's really all it is: an idea. It is no more necessary to immortality than boobs on a bull. Animus is all around you. Trying to get it from blood is rather like trying to extract water from a rock while standing in a lake.

These are *my* definitions. If you are true to yourself, you may not even choose to call your twin a vampire. Perhaps she is more akin to the fae or the dark-and-winged-ones. What's important is to create your Other with the *power* and the *motivation* to teach you. What's important is to create your Other to love you beyond all others, so that she is sufficiently motivated to take upon itself the grave responsibility of "turning" you.

Clearly, for anyone who is a forward thinker, this can begin to stray into the darker alleys of the darker teachings, so I will leave it here for now, with the strong reiteration that your Other is who *you* need him/her to be. Whether she is a vampire, that is entirely up to you.

As an afterthought, many seekers choose the word vampire because the traditional myths are deeply ingrained into world culture. This *can* have the effect of providing impetus to one's own agendas. It is a matter of using the *power* of the consensus without falling prey to the *myths* of the consensus. The power of the vampire myth is that it centers around immortality and a shadow world co-existing and overlapping the so-called real world. We call that Otherworld vampireland, but it could just as easily be known by any other name.

Using the Program Against Itself

> *You mentioned that it is possible to "use the power of the consensus without bowing to the myths of the consensus." I assume that one could use the power of the consensus to do more than form one's ideal image of the twin. Perhaps, to, say, disseminate information or gather like-minded individuals to The Path or what have you, in order to destroy the program itself from within?*

Study tales of "the jester." If you are going to go up against the consensus (for example – "attempting to disseminate information or gather like-minded individuals to the path"), sometimes the only way to do it is to knowingly and intentionally make a fool of yourself in front of the king and all his horses. If you attempt to take a more direct path to your goal, you may find your head staring up at your neck from the floor. The jester (aka "the fool") takes it upon himself or herself to make the king laugh while the other subjects in the audience might be *seeing* deeper into the jester's antics than the king (who is blinded by power and self-importance.)

On the flip side of the coarse fabric of reality, study Machiavelli's "The Prince." While the jester works with comedy and irony, the prince is instructed to rule through fear and respect. There is something to be said for either one, but there is seldom if ever much common ground between the two. So it depends largely on your personal proclivities – are you the jester or the prince?

I've recently been thinking about how all-pervasive the Program is and how some people see it for what it is but can only, at this point, try to subvert it by working within it. For example, some people are trying to bring to the attention of Congress evidence that the U.S. military has been, for decades, covering up viable technology that would free everyone from using oil and coal resources. These people want Congress to order a disclosure of these technologies. Unfortunately, no one is taking these people and their evidence seriously, a direct result of the Program's insidious influence, for sure.

Those technologies have existed for decades, if not longer. I've noticed that Tesla's ideas are making a come-back, but it is doubtful they will get a foothold for the simple reason that they would disempower the oil companies overnight if implemented. There was a short-lived series not long ago called *Dracula* (appropriately enough) wherein Drac had become a steampunk sorcerer, but his technologies were subverted and ultimately destroyed. Unfortunately, the series suffered a similar fate, but it was an interesting look at the kind of conspiracy theory you mentioned. And personally, I've lived long enough to know that it *is* a conspiracy and not just a theory.

Is using the power of the consensus without succumbing to its myths a dangerous game for a seeker? And, one last thing, can you give another example of using the power of the consensus against itself?

Yes, it is a dangerous game. A very dangerous game. You talk about disseminating information, just for one example.

186

My website is actually quite tame as these things go, but I have received numerous threats as a result of its existence, and the publisher has been harassed numerous times.

Agent Smith is not only alive and well, so is Big Brother. And as paranoid as this may sound, they really are out to get you. But, yes. I say it again. It is a very dangerous game.

I knew a lady once who decided to use the power of the consensus (in particular the archetype) to create and manifest her Other. She chose the common paradigm of *Dracula* – in particular the film which starred Frank Langella. She focused on these images and summoned the power of the consensus to hone her idea of what her twin should look and be like – an immortal being with the ability to pass that immortality along to her.

Time went by, other things took precedence, and she more or less stopped doing the active summoning, though her Intent never waned. One evening near dusk, she looked out to see a horse-drawn carriage in front of her house. She lived in a rural area, but such a contraption was out of place as well as seemingly out of time. She went out to see what was happening, only to discover the carriage was empty, the door open as if someone had disembarked, but no one was about. When she tried to take the horse by the reins, it began to run, and soon disappeared into the darkness – not unlike the horse-drawn carriage Dracula had used in the film.

She never found who owned the carriage, never saw it again, but it came to be her belief that it had delivered her Other to her in accordance with her intent. To put it in your language, she built the image of her twin and her Intent took that image beyond the myths.

It's just a story she likes to tell, but I personally believe it to be true.

If nothing in the world has any real meaning, what reason would a seeker have to do anything other than create the twin and transmogrify? Makes everything but the path seem a completely meaningless waste of time and energy, and yet, on we go. I feel at this point that I'm delving into an awkward form of fundamentalism.

In some ways, everything *is* the path. It is The Life. But life is for living, so it is only when the seeker *becomes* the path that she realizes there is no separation of the self from the journey. So many who first embark on this journey are still fragmented. They believe there is the dayshine self and the immortal self – but ultimately, both are the same. There is only one world, divided infinitely by perception. When the seeker begins to experience herself as the one world instead of the division is when the seeker has become the path instead of only trying to be *on* the path.

My frustration comes from feeling like I am not asking the right questions. I need to go further. I feel like I'm in the movie Dark City, *wandering a labyrinthine box I can't escape.*

When you feel the need to go further, it is generally time to throw away all the maps and books and gurus you've encountered along the way, and embrace the fact that the only thing left to do is to draw your own maps and write your own books and call upon your own inner guru, who is probably the one shouting in your ear that you are only a character wandering a labyrinthine box.

You really can't escape the box. You can only be *beyond* the box. There is no process. As Yoda once told me by a campfire on the shores of Hell, "Do or do not. There is no try."

The only process that *might* exist is the work the seeker has done to reach this point. There is simply a moment – from one moment to the next – wherein the seeker is suddenly outside the box enough to realize she was never *in* the box all along. She *is* the box. That is the moment when you have the opportunity to seize the tiller of creation, smash the box from the inside out, and fly free.

Beyond Religion

Most religions have at their core a gram or two of truth. Reason being – most religions were founded on actual Knowledge. In the case of Christianity, most of the core beliefs stem from what Jesus supposedly said – which means one man reasoned it out and the rest jumped on the bandwagon. I want to make it absolutely clear that no one can do the work for you – no, not even Jesus or god. Not even your Other. The one who does the work of self-actualization is you, yourself and *you*.

I personally do not like the word "faith" because in our current culture it has come to mean something other than what was originally intended. *Real* faith is actually Intent that is manifested by words and actions combined. And yet, the way most religious folk use the word, it comes to mean, simply, "belief." And what someone believes is entirely irrelevant and absolutely disempowering unless and until those beliefs are put into action.

Some have asked, "What action, Mikal? What should I be do-ing?"

That's not for me to answer. What creates and manifests the Other is not any pat recipe.

The ache and longing
which lie outside of me
are portals and windows
to the hunger within.
I-Am
that which is
the pixels and dreams of
the cry in the night,
the voice of the twin,
screaming
"I–Am."

That's *my* truth. Your mileage will vary.

Becoming One with the inner teacher is inhabiting the totality of oneself and achieving what Christianity refers to as "the holy trinity."

Mortal Self
Immortal Other
Conjoined Singularity

In Biblical terms, these attributes were assigned to God alone, but in reality this is the very structure of the human soul – it is a 3-part entity which begins with the mortal human, evolves to the projected Immortal Other, and culminates in the (re)conjoining of the two, at which point a transformation, transcendence or transmogrification is Willed into being, resulting in the infinite Singularity.

This is the core nature of the holy trinity – it didn't come into being through religion. Quite the contrary. It is a facet of *nature* which has been skewed by religion until it has left humans believing they are "wretches" who need to be saved through "amazing grace." In reality, *you* are the trinity.

The thing about allowing the impossible is that it really isn't a natural thing for most humans to do. It's called "the impossible" because it's part of The Program that tells you something can't be done. *Even if you have rejected 99.9% of that program, the .01% still remaining is like a hologram – it is the <u>whole</u> thing even though it is but a fragment. Knowing that is the only tool you have for getting beyond it.*

Examine your own belief matrix, and you will find that certain things have been filed under the category of impossible, largely as a result of your conditioning. You would say it is impossible to fly, for example, yet you do it in Dreaming, and certain mystics or shamans may levitate or even fly within their biological forms – which, of course, are not really biological at all

You may believe it is impossible to become transformed while in corporeal form, again because that is the programming with which you have been fitted within the consensus. Turn your mind around and look at it like this: it is commonly believed even among spiritual adepts that transformation occurs at death because most spiritual adepts accept that program and, in doing so, wait around to die. Yes, the transformation you seek *might* occur at death, because then there is no alternative, if it is to occur at all. And yet, it is a humanform belief that tells you it is necessary to die first. The most difficult death you will ever experience is the one while you are still alive.

> *So it's a shift of the assemblage point. Like the holy men who walk through fiery furnaces without being consumed, with no ill effects. Certainly that is some sort of movement of the assemblage point, too, right?*

Yes.

What you are seeking, however – complete and lasting transformation – is a shift of the assemblage point that would not allow for a complete return to ordinary awareness. That is why fear and doubt stop most humans from ever making the attempt – and so they follow the course of least resistance, accepting their transformation only after going through the humanform act of dying.

It's the last paragraph that really spills the cat out of the beanery. I have highlighted the pertinent comment. To simplify, this kind of transformation lies beyond the perceptual range of the human organism, so it falls squarely into the category of not just the unknown but the Unknowable. That being the case, what has to happen is a fundamental alteration of the organism itself – an expansion of perception and awareness which recreate the organism as something other-than-human. That is the foundation of transmogrification.

I can deal with more physical pain than most. But there are times that I reach my mental limit. Obviously no one wants to live in an "extended longevity" scenario with chronic debilitating pain.

This is precisely why I encourage seekers to strive for the highest level of transformation – which is transmogrification. The transmogrified individual is no longer in a biological matrix at all, and so physical pain is not part of the equation.

In *The Matrix*, Morpheus says to Neo, "Do you think that's air you're breathing?"

Have you ever seen something that you really can't wrap your mind around? A ghost, for example? If so, did you notice the machinations your mind went through in an attempt to categorize and explain and therefore dismiss the event? The human mind creates limitations for itself so as to have parameters in which to operate. One of the most obvious is time. When you can release the limitations, your world automatically expands.

Believe something is impossible, and it is then impossible.

If an immortal were standing right in front of you, would you perceive him at all, or would your mind reject the idea entirely because, "That's impossible!"? Another clue as to why vampires are said to have no reflection – humans can't see what they cannot perceive.

Allowing the impossible is a subtle transformation and cannot be forced. It can only be *permitted*. Softly. Did you ever see those pixilated 3-D images that were popular back in the 1980s? If you look at it with your normal vision, it looks like nothing more than a bunch of random pixels. But if you can move your eyes from side to side (shift your perception), out pops a 3-D doo-dad of some sort – a dolphin, a starship, a pumpkin. That's impossible... but there it is, just a different way of looking at the equation. Some people see the 3-D doo-dad almost immediately. Others stare at it for hours before it pops out at them. Still others never see it at all.

Spirit, Mind, Body

Transformation, transcension, transmogrification – each is a different sort of evolution, and each is accessible within the span of the seeker's mortal lifetime. In other words, unlike Darwinian evolution which requires dozens of generations (minimally) for evolution to occur, the immortal evolution is something that can be intended and willed by a fundamental rearranging of the spirit/mind/body. I put it in that order, because in my experience, that is the order in which any self-willed evolution occurs. Here's why:

1. Spirit. It is often spirit that transforms first. You may know who and what you are in spirit long before your mind and body are willing to get on board.

2. Mind. Once the seeker hears the call of spirit (or the voice of the Other, if you prefer) Mind begins to niggle at the problem and goes on its many searches for answers.

3. Body. Because the body is comprised of what we mistakenly believe to be organic heavy matter, it is the last to accept and allow transmogrification. The reasons for this are many – not the least of which is fear. The body mistakenly believes it is all, when the reality is that it is the lowest on the totem pole – but try telling *it* that!

In most cases, spirit and mind transform or transmogrify long before body. If body never gets on board, then transcension may occur at the time of mortal death.

Why Can't We Just Shoot the Messenger?

Seems to me that a lot of so-called teachers should be avoided at all costs. I'm thinking of Aleister Crowley, Anton Levey, and even Carlos Castaneda. I know a lot of seekers will disagree, but it just seems to me that when something is <u>too</u> radical, it loses all credibility.

As for Crowley and Levey, I'm not at all an expert on their lives, nor do I think it's necessary to examine the messenger too closely. Some of the very best and wisest teachers throughout history have been "madmen" if you examine their personal lives or their later years spent in dementia. You mentioned Carlos Castaneda, so I'll use him as an example, since I am more familiar with his works.

If you read his books and study *The Teachings of Don Juan*, you will find a workable system of knowledge that's whole and complete unto itself. In fact, it is my contention that don Juan *was* Carlos's alter-ego or – double/Other/twin. That aside, many people have tried to debunk Castaneda because, in his later years, he became even more of a recluse and had what amounted to a harem of several women. He had taught celibacy. He had spoken against indulgence. His teachings focused on the austere. Worse – he had said in his teachings that a man could "leave this earth in the manner of a sorcerer" and leave no body behind.

And then he died.

His followers were stunned. How could he *die*? He was an immortal sorcerer!

And yet, he never claimed that, and in fact had said many times he believed he would not succeed in his bid for transmogrification – which was really what he was talking about without using the word – and that he would die a normal death and reach his double through what amounted to transcension.

So it would *seem* that Carlos taught the masses through his books, but lost his way in his later years. However, what's worth examining is the realization that the man and the teachings are often not of the same world in the least. Why? Because often the teachings may be coming from one's Other while the body is still comprised of human flesh and bone, and therefore vulnerable to disease, decay, dementia, and death.

And yet, for anyone who takes a closer look, you'll often discover that the teachings are sound even if the teacher isn't. That's just the way of it – and it is one of the ways the consensus reality protects its own status quo. Humans feel if they can discredit the messenger, then they are freed from any responsibility to the message. To this day, there are entire organizations dedicated to the debunking of Castaneda. Rather ironic when you think about it, as these organizations were founded by Castaneda's former apprentices. When "the man" died, it sent a lot of his followers into a tailspin because they couldn't reconcile that the man was *not* the teachings. He was just the messenger. And they shot him post mortem (well, figuratively).

As to Levey and Crowley, it really doesn't matter who they were as human beings. What matters is what they brought forth as Knowledge. I'll also say that Satanism is just an offshoot of Christianity – to believe in the devil you would have to believe in the Christian God, since that is where the devil originates and reigns supreme. This is another reason I have discouraged seekers from becoming Satanists – it just promotes a backassward belief in God, which must then be eradicated along with all other false belief systems.

What I advise is generally this: be a raven in nature. Steal from all the other birds, whatever shiny tidbit of knowledge appeals to you. But leave the nest in the rearview mirror. And, yes, I include my own teachings in this.

Take what you need, leave the rest, fly free.

Creating a Creator:
The Potential Power of Grief

Is loss something immortals experience? Should it be cultivated, accepted, eliminated, or embraced? Is it a petty emotion like anger? Is it a strength?

The answers to your questions depend largely on what has been lost to you. As an example, if you are referring to the loss of a relationship in high school, as contrasted against the death of a long-time lover and companion, the answers would be quite different.

It has been my experience that immortals experience loss more deeply than any other creature, because the loss is actually eternal. There are no typically human thoughts of, *We'll meet again,* or *I know you'll be with me always.* The immortal, more than any other, Knows these are not realistic sentiments, since the gulf between life and death is as wide and deep as the void itself.

As such, this kind of grief can and often does serve as the impetus to become what is known as a "creator" – one who has the ability to "turn" others toward their own immortality. So in that regard, it can be a strength, although one with an ironic root system.

At that level, it is certainly not a petty emotion. The only way to nurture it is to go to war against the brute with the scythe – to *see* him as the arrogant bastard son of a god who creates magnificent beings, only to make them mortal and prone to decay, pain and death.

It matters not in the least whether you believe such myths or not. What matters is the awareness that mortality is only the yin that exists in direct opposition to the yang. In that regard, grief can be a strength, but it is a strength that comes with tremendous and often crushing responsibility.

This is precisely why most humans would prefer to accept their mortality rather than waking to the realization that all things have their opposite, but it is only through extreme measures that grief can be turned into the life-giving animus of immortality.

Becoming a creator is not something that occurs through passivity, but through relentless Intent and all but debilitating grief. Such is the nature of opposites.

You will never understand what I am about to tell you if you approach it from the human perspective, because it is not something that can be understood in any traditional sense, nor is it human by definition, but must be absorbed through the osmosis of gnosis and covertly perused from the far side of the bridge, knowing all the while that any bridge exists and simultaneously does not exist, depending entirely on the where-when one is standing in relation to the transmutating bridge outside any consensual idea of Time.

Ah, but before we begin to unravel such conundrums, I must remind you that how you think of yourself in relation to these things is going to determine how or *if* you will ever grasp the handlebars of the roller coaster that disembarks from the realm of humanity and leads straight to what most would see as insanity, but which is in actuality the heart of vampireland and immortality.

> *The danger is that you have come to believe there are levels of reality and some innate hierarchy of worlds, when the only truth is what I have said before: there is only one world, divided infinitely by perception.*

But now it is time for the more advanced lesson, in which I tell you that it is those divisions in perception which create the illusion of otherworlds, and each and every perception is going to determine not only *what* you see, but *how* you interpret it, and the interpretation is going to determine whether you will choose to experience those worlds or only maintain them as distant fantasies upon which you may

197

dream because you have chosen to perceive them as unattainable.

If you see vampireland as something that only exists beyond the event horizon of death, then that is what it will be, and the only way inside the kingdom will involve dying to get in, see? And while that is as real as anything else in the grand scheme of All Things, it is not the only possibility, and the danger is that it takes some measure of choice away from you and places it in the hands of random phantom Chance, so again I would caution you to reconsider your mindset lest it keep you from embracing the higher truth which is the soul-deep understanding of the statement: every reality is created with a thought.

If you think I am "out there", then that is where you have placed me. If you believe vampireland is only accessible through the cemetery gates, then so shall it be, as above so below, yes?

The immortal's trick is to *be* what he *thinks*, and to think before believing, and to be always questioning reality in a way that goes beyond merely observing what *appears* to be, and examining the underlying mechanism that is responsible for spinning all things into various states of *Being*. And it is through that examination that you begin to confront those structural underpinnings which answer to the arbitrary labels of time, light, gravity and antimatter, and how it is in the end the manipulation of them that will open the only door that exists between "here" and vampireland.

The human paradigm is built on the false notion of Time, and so it could be observed by one outside the matrix that the entire paradigm itself is erroneous because it has created within its subjects a viewpoint that is based on what immortals call The First Fundamental Lie. And yet, because you have always existed within the confines of The Lie, how does one undo a lifetime of belief when that belief has long since been ingrained as truth?

It is one thing to undo the programs that make you human, but another thing entirely to unfasten the precepts that are fundamental to your notion of what it means to be *human* – essentially what you have come to accept as 'human abilities' and 'human limitations'.

Think on this, for it is only when you are willing to sacrifice The Lie that you will be able to glimpse these elementary elements of creation which are channeled through your essential being pure and limitless, but restricted entirely by The Lie which was seemingly designed to do just that.

> *Ironic, yes? You are made of the pixels and photons of limitlessness and timelessness, yet unable to access that nature because the nature of any consensus is to create parameters which can only limit the power and understanding of the thing itself.*

And yet, here is the secret you have yet to *Realize*, contained in the question: *Who* is creating the consensus? The mirror doesn't lie.

The Effect of Practicality on Magick

Militant practicality is the death of spontaneous magic.

If you find yourself thinking too hard about what you should or shouldn't do because this or that may or may not be possible according to the laws of physics, thermodynamics and logic, you will quickly discover that the magic you had planned to do has left the building in favor of more temperate climes.

Magic does not thrive because of practicality, *but in spite of it.*

Time After Time

Couldn't you travel forward in time to whenever you wanted?

Within the hologram of time, everything that has ever been or ever will be is already recorded. So, yes, immortals are not constrained by the linear illusion of time. Neither are mortals, but the difference is that most immortals realize this, while most humans do not. The universe isn't really dying because it isn't really alive to begin with. It is a stage and a milieu upon which countless trillions of beings go through the motions of Life.

If you want to be scared out of your wits, consider this: it would *appear* on the surface to be a pattern, acted out Time after Time on the stage of the infinite, like a Broadway play running for years, so long that the actors forget they are actors and become the characters they set out to play. But what I have *seen* is that there are other holograms, in which it is possible to break the pattern and *be* another version of who you think you are.

That's why you need to be able to answer the question: "Who *are* you?" because if you go jumping from one hologram to another, it's easy to lose your foundational foundation, and when that happens there will be a great fall into the abyss and no amount of frog kisses will be able to put humpty dumpty together again (or something like that fairy's tail which lies at the root of all human believings.)

It could be conceived that immortals are a part of the energetic structure of the universe, but moving between the quantum particles and waves of light, so as to be unaffected by the gravity of time itself.

> *Time, when viewed from the human perspective, could be understood to be an erosive and corrosive element, the antithesis to Life far more than even the idea of mortal Death.*

That which is eternal is eternal because that which is eternal does not exist within the limitations and confines of linear time. Immortals recognize that time is a gauge developed for the convenience of humans.

As I've said previously, the truly ironic thing about immortals (including vampires) is that we are beings of light. Things traveling at the speed of light do not obey the rules of time as it is commonly (mis)understood.

Time is the dark gravity that manifests mortality.

Christ Consciousness

I keep running into the term 'Christ Consciousness'. What is it?

The term is generally used in new age circles to indicate that someone is like Christ in their way of thinking and living. This presumes that Christ ever really lived (highly debatable) and that he was somehow exalted in his thinking. Personally, I am inclined to think that he was simply someone who walked the path, perhaps with the assistance of allies and power plants, but certainly not because he was the son of any god.

Perhaps the myth might serve as inspiration to some. But when people start expecting Christ to save them or intervene in their daily lives or allow their team to win that football game, they are just sadly deluded sheeple.

I do not strive to have Christ consciousness. I strive to have self-awareness and an unshakable *I-Am*. Anything less is following in someone else's footsteps and fading into their shadow.

Be who *you* are.

That's what Jesus would do.

Stop Talking To Yourself!

Many say it's important to have positive self-talk and be cognizant of the way you talk to yourself, while Della Van Hise, for example, makes it clear the inner dialog should be eliminated altogether because it never has anything useful to say. Is thinking in words less effective than images or feelings? Am I confusing self-talk with the inner dialog?

How can you hear the voice of your twin if you are forever talking to yourself?

Most of the time the internal dialog is nothing more than lists, mindless observations (emphasis on "mindless") and self-judgments. Therefore, it is good to learn to eliminate it because it is really nothing more than the voice of the consensus, the chatter of the hive mind manifesting in your own personal language. Self-talk and the internal dialog are the same thing (as far as I am concerned... and I am always right.)

Silent knowing is where you will hear the voice of the Other, or the voice of gnosis. Not all gnosis necessarily comes from your twin, but all of gnosis passes *through* your twin. Yes, it is a paradox. (But I am never wrong.)

When you can learn how to move through life with a permanent connection to gnosis is when you be moving with Intent in the direction of your personal evolution. The internal dialog will lie to you all day long. The voice of gnosis always speaks truth – sometimes in words, sometimes in symbols, sometimes in silence.

It should also be observed that the sweet wind of gnosis might occasionally distort the truth. It may outright lie – though lies are often truths spoken outside of time. Meaning, it would have appeared to be a lie in the year 1125 to say "The Earth is round." Now it appears to be a lie to say "The Earth is flat." One day it will be a lie to say "The Earth is an object in space." Truth is not relative to time, but perception can be relative to truth.

When the voice of gnosis might appear to lead you astray, it is usually because your Other is forcing you to move beyond the sum of your parts, and outside the matrix of your human abilities. This is where real evolution occurs.

The internal dialog will have plenty to say about this. None of it will be good. *Chitty-chitty-chat-chat-you-are-a-silly-sod-of-a-bastard-go-back-to-church-go-back-to-school-return-to-yo-mama's-teat-for-you-are-out-of-your-league-and-deluded-to-boot-it's-just-an-easy-stroll-from-cradle-to-grave-so-stop-standing-there-pondering-your-crusty-navel-and-go-to-hell-where-all-your-friends-and-family-are-waiting-with-wine-and-roses-to-welcome-you-home.*

The internal dialog generally speaks in the voice of a dung beetle, just for reference.

Are you saying that all mental speech is internal dialog? Is thinking largely useless then?

Most wordy conversations that occur in the mind are just internal dialog. There are exceptions, such as when one has a quantum leap and suddenly understands something that was previously obscure. This often occurs in words, though more often in conceptual graphics.

Thinking is another matter altogether. When you are actively thinking, you are using a process of assimilation – putting things together to form a mosaic of knowledge, or at least a pathway of information that might one day lead to knowledge.

Examples:

Internal dialog: "It's a nice today. But is it ever *really* nice? I mean look at that fat man over there on the bench. Is that you in 20 years? And what about that guy you pissed off yesterday. Do you think he'll hunt you down and try to hurt you? Don't forget – we need to load up on condoms because it's uncle's day at the bunny ranch and..."

Thinking: "If I want to achieve the art of transmogrification, there are many things I am going to need to change in how I look at life. Do I believe all things die? (stopping here to ponder the question). If I do believe it, then is my own mind/body/spirit working against me in my bid for immortality? By believing all things die, have I already condemned myself to a final dance with Death? And if I do believe it, how might I go about *un*believing it? Are there examples in nature of things that don't die? What about rumors of immortals living among us? Would validating immortality help me in my own bid to attain it?"

As you can see, the internal dialog is random and generally chaotic. It's just your "character" talking to himself to fill the silence. Thinking is what occurs *within* the silence.

Energy Vampires

At some level, it could be argued that all beings are energy vampires. What must be considered is why anyone would want to feed on the energy of other human beings, when energy is abundant throughout the universe, and may be gleaned directly from the four organic elements – earth, air, fire, water – in addition to the four inorganic elements: time, light, gravity, antimatter. The seeker who learns to feed on earth/air/fire/water strengthens their chi in the organic world. The seeker who learns to feed on time/light/gravity/antimatter strengthens their essence in the inorganic world. The seeker who feeds on other humans... well... not much to be said for that.

204

A lot of folks want the idea of power that comes from calling themselves a psychic vampire. Nothing wrong with that in and of itself – but for anyone truly seeking to evolve, I would highly recommend learning to feed off the animus of the universe at large.

Remember: all things are energy. And yet, the energy one would take from others is *not* particularly pure, and is probably *more* difficult to absorb *because* it is energy-in-use (in manifestation) as opposed to energy-at-large (that which is unmanifest).

Think of it this way: why would you want to drink from a bottle of water when you were standing in the middle of a pure, clean waterfall?

The most *real* energy vampires I have encountered are those who stay up late figuring out ways to get other people to do things for them, support them, do their work. The resulting loss of energy from the host is phenomenal – I mean this literally. Energy vampires are also "kids in capes" – wannabe little idjits who sit around in a dark room burning black candles and chanting the devil's prayer in Latin because they once saw it on an episode of Buffy. This kind of would-be energy vampire is harmless, but nonetheless annoying for its contribution to human stupidity.

> *Energy vampires are all around you – but they are mortal misfits and have nothing to do with immortality.*

If you want to learn to take animus from the universe at large, study some basic breathing techniques, particularly those associated with tai chi. This is one of the easiest ways to take energy from the world at large, though there are other ways that work just as well. Meditation. Martial arts *kata*. Immersion in nature. Tantric sex.

Another way to generate energy and uptake animus is to scare yourself limp. That's a slightly more complex technique, but occasionally worth it if you have a strong heart. When you are caught in the throes of genuine fear for your life, a state of mind ensues that has been described as stopping time. The world around you starts to resemble a slow motion scene in an action movie, and your mind is sped up like a train racing toward the sanctuary of a station. The end result is that you are able to think faster than time is moving, and are therefore likely to come up with an immediate solution to your seemingly imminent demise.

While one may *appear* on the surface to have nothing to do with one another, what is actually happening is that mind, body, and spirit are downloading the infinite amount of animus it will require to step out of the path of that oncoming bus or dodge the bullet that has your name inscribed on it in perfect calligraphy. And while I would not recommend intentionally placing yourself in that kind of danger, it cannot be denied that the results are phenomenal with regard to the increase in energy, strength and vitality one feels in the aftermath of escaping Death.

In so very many ways, the vampire mythos parallels the shenanigans of human nature. Most humans feed off of "zombieland" in one way or another – whether they are plugged into the comforting blue teat of the television or mindlessly following some religious or political agenda – *they* are the zombies without ever realizing when or how they got turned.

True immortals feed from pure energy – which is all around us and need not be gleaned from unsuspecting teenage girl who is more vapid than a bag of rocks. Empty calories at best.

> *Is it not possible to be self-perpetuating? Dynamic energy – life within life? Somewhat like a torus. A sovereign being – one who doesn't need to take but self-generates from within.*

Good question – to which the answer is *yes*, that is the highest state of transmogrification, but since it is a state that is generally achieved and mastered long after one transmogrifies, I tend to focus more along the lines of "getting there" as opposed to "being there." For most seekers, there are stages of transformation, and at most of those stages, some manner of sustenance (maintenance) is required – though not at the level you are speaking of. At that level, sustenance comes entirely from the self-renewing energy, which one is continuously self-regenerating.

In *Teachings of the Immortals*, there is a sketch illustrating how a transmogrified individual essentially moves in and out of the non-local web of energy, whereas a mortal exists is a more segregated and separated state of being (known as organic matter).

The way to attain such a condition is through awareness that all things are truly energy at a fundamental level. Humans tend to separate themselves from the universe, believing they are autonomous – a segregated organism that lives and dies a solitary experience. The reality, of course – for humans *and* immortals – is that there is no difference between the man gazing at the stars, and the stars themselves.

Animal Spirit

Do animals have souls and if so is it possible for them to evolve past their furry little meat suits? I'd also like to ask: Mikal, do you have a definitive or absolute view on death itself? Why does it seem that everything lives just to die?

My definitive and absolute view on death itself is very simple: it is a flaw in the program, a virus that has disrupted the natural order until it has become the new normal. At times I have seen it almost as a sentient entity, though that is only the personality put onto it by humans who overlay their beliefs onto things they do not understand. The unfortunate result is that people accept death as part of what they euphemistically call "the cycle of life."

When a seeker becomes a seer, it is clearly *seen* (if one has the courage to look – which is rare even among seers) that death is not natural. But now that it is so heavily entwined into the human matrix, just as a virus entwines itself into the root programming and root directory at times, it may be that the only way to get rid of it is either a complete system reboot (planet-wide), or through individual re-booting (transmogrification).

With that said, regarding animals, I have no doubt that they have the same kind of living animus as humans. I do not usually refer to it as a soul, but more of an essence that is unique to the creature itself (whether animal or human). As to whether they can evolve, I have no definitive answer. I want-to-believe they are *already* more evolved than humans, but that is putting humanform beliefs onto non-human entities, no?

I will just say this: the animals I have known personally lived their lives fully and always in the Now, and when they left this world, they left a large empty space where that essence used to be. I would say that is evidence (at least subjective and personal) that they were more than the sum of their mortal parts.

How Dead is Dead?

Can one save a person from death once they have died?

Before this question could really be answered, you would need to define what is meant by "died" and what is meant by "save". If you are talking about raising someone from the dead, as in the Biblical fable of Lazarus, I would have to say that it would be a bad idea for a lot of reasons. There is nothing to say it can't be done, but the old monkey-paw questions automatically spring to mind. Would it be the same person at all? Would we need to call the zombie squad?

In my own experience, if you are moving through linear time as 99.999% of humans are, then dead is dead and it is permanent.

> *If time is not real, can we bend the laws of time and go back to a time when they were still alive? Can we still save them? Do immortals have an infinite amount of time to eventually save someone?*

From a quantum perspective, time is not a progressive series of events leading from past to present to future. It might be best understood as spherical, but even that is misleading. Put as simply as possible, time is a hologram. Everything that will ever happen has already happened, which is also why the big bang and the big collapse are simply mirror images of one another. The upside is that it enables those who know how to navigate the hologram to move in and out of what is commonly thought of as time. The downside is that it *appears* to condemn us (all of us, including immortals) to an always-repeating cycle. There was a television series not long ago called *True Detective*. From it came some quotes worthy of note.

> 1. *"Fuck, I don't want to know anything anymore. This is a world where nothing is solved. Someone once told me, 'Time is a flat circle.' Everything we've ever done or will do, we're gonna do over and over and over again. And that little boy and that little girl, they're gonna be in that room again and again and again forever."*
>
> –*True Detective*
> A rant by Rust Cohle

There is some dark truth to that – something I have previously avoided including in *The Darker Teachings* for obvious reasons. The universe breathes in and it breathes out. We would all like to believe that each breath brings new possibilities, but occasional glimpses of *deja vu* more or less confirm that you have been here before and you will be here again. But really, it is all the same breath. I could elaborate on this, and perhaps I should, but I've found that humans need *some* manner of illusion just to take their next breath, which might be the same ailment from which the universe itself is suffering.

> 2. *"Death created Time to grow the things that it would kill."*
>
> –True Detective

When I first heard that line of dialog, I could not help thinking I could have written it myself. And I have. Death is the hag-bride of time. Time is the nagging wife of Death.

> *It's a lot of pain to worry about someone's death, but once it's over, is it really over?*

A better question might be – is everyone (scientists, doctors, et al) looking in the wrong direction? Are they trying to cure illness to buy more time, when perhaps they need to be looking at what *causes* time and death in the first place.

Is it really over? In linear time, yes. In holographic time, changes can be affected, but when the universe rolls over in her bed, things tend to play out much as they ever did, or seemingly ever will.

Sorry if that seems dark or without hope, and I can only hope I am wrong. You may step back into the lifetime of someone who has died (if you know how to navigate holographic time), but generally any changes you make only reverse themselves due to the "imprint" of time upon the hologram itself. In other words, save someone from being struck dead by a bus, and they will step out in front of the

210

same bus yesterday. No other explanation is possible. And you would be highly encouraged to prove me wrong.

We try to save others from death, and what's it for? Without being free of the program myself yet, I don't even have that power. I do, but I'm not sure I could summon it when the time came.

Your only obligation to yourself is to do what you Will. Expect nothing. If it is important for you to pursue that path, then you will do so, one way or another. It will depend largely on the depth of your grief and the power of your relentless Intent.

I hope by posing multiple questions you understand the general intent behind what I am asking. I've seen your responses on the forum that going back in time is possible, but seekers have experienced it being like a movie.

If you look at it from purely mortal time, and if you learn to navigate holographic time, then you may be able to experience stepping back inside the lifetime of someone you love who has died. But can you *save* them? I have not found that to be the case. What I have observed is that a lifetime tends to be a finite unite of measure (a life inside X-amount of time).

So if you were to revisit your Great Uncle Ulrich during the span of his life, you might be able to sit down together and discuss the weather over a cup of tea, but even if you could cure the cancer that ultimately intends to kill him on March 3, 1992, observation shows he will still die on that same date and at the same time, but of a fatal heart attack or pulmonary embolism. For reasons not clearly understood even by the immortals, once something is consigned to the archive of the hologram, it cannot be resurrected into *current* time.

That isn't to say it *can't* be done. It is only saying that none I know have been able to accomplish it. *Yet.* They are never truly gone, for their imprint also exists within the hologram. They are always alive *within* the hologram, *within* their natural lifetime. What might be gone is the ability to extend their awareness beyond the span of that natural lifetime. This is why I stress the importance of doing what you can *while* you can.

There is no single right answer. We move through time with the awareness that we are swimming in a dream that has swallowed the world. What exists beyond the dream? The thing that swallowed it.

One reason I have never discussed this at length is because it is virtually impossible to expand upon. Free will exists, but so does determinism (side by side, as a fully functional duality). Determinism exists, and free will is the force of Will which can overcome determinism, thereby placing one essentially outside the box. Determinism exists in what you might call "the big picture" (the big bang, the big collapse). Free Will exists within the hologram of Now.

I could say that some things are hard-wired into the fabric of the universe's existence, but that would only sound like determinism to you. What determines determinism? Free will determines determinism. If you *see* that, it will make sense. If you don't, keep looking.

Some things cannot be understood with intellect alone. They must be experienced within the hologram of the Dream. If you want to understand the duality of free will and determinism, learn to Dream the hologram. It may not answer all your questions, but it will give you a broader perspective for seeing.

So time isn't a lie in and of itself, just the way we perceive/measure time is a lie? And we're subject to a holographic time/universe wherein we're destined to repeat the same actions over and over even as immortals? Or is free will going to break us out of this cycle?

Time is still the first fundamental lie. It does not exist as an entity unto itself. It is simply how humans measure and categorize events. What you are trying to bust yourself out of is the *illusion* of time and the gravity it leaves in its wake – i.e., time is death and death is time, but both are illusions within the matrix. The immortal condition is attained when one inhabits the assemblage point of the Other – essentially an energetic structure that is not subject to the savage ravages of time and death. Both time and death are *non*-energies. They are *non*-entities, and so to defeat them is to become the antithesis of them, no?

When I am talking about the universe breathing in and breathing out, it is such a *very* big picture that it is hardly relevant to any individuated being. To deny it would be pointless. To acknowledge it is almost equally as pointless – only because even most immortals have difficulty wrapping their mind around the distance between each big bang and each big collapse[24].

It's one of those things that seekers need to look at from the corner of the third eye – because when you look at it straight on, it tends to either disappear altogether (because humans are programmed to consider time an absolute), or it will shift form into some massive conundrum.

The problem with a duality (time/death or free-will/determinism) is that it has certain parallels to the double-slit experiment wherein it is observed that light is both particle and wave. With regard to just the concept of time it depends largely which slit one is looking through.

---

[24] When I use terms such as "big bang" and "big collapse," keep in mind I am not a physicist, and the terms I employ are used to create a mental picture rather than a scientific map of the life and death of the universe.

> *Look through one slit, and time will appear as a flat sheet covering the universe. Look through the other, and it will appear as an idea in the mind of a mad frog.*

Where time is concerned, the seeker's greatest task is to step outside of it altogether – so that the thing being observed is not seen through either slit, but from an altogether different mindset which is the perspective of the Other.

The universe is a deterministic block of space-time, in that everything from every point in time to every other point in time is already written. However, free will is used to shift or alter the block at will, with the caveat being that you are not just acting at the point in time that you currently perceive, you are actually altering (potentially) every point in time by using your free will "now" (since "now" is every point in time).

There is a question as to whether free will alters the block of space-time, or if it only alters the *perception* and experience of the individuated organism. As there is no way to test this in any practical manner, I can only speculate that I would prefer to extend the life of a rose in the garden as opposed to watching it wilt and dry on my forgotten altar.

The so-called big bang may be what caused time in the first place (or at least the need to perceive the illusion of the first fundamental lie). I mention this only because some quantum physics wizards I know have toyed with the idea of – "What would happen if the big bang never happened?" Based on data too complex to even begin to impart here, their conclusion is that the matter-energy contained within the big bang may actually be what happened when the big bang didn't happen. All of time was captured within that blob of matter-energy (which was no larger than a grain of sand, it was so tightly compacted) and when it exploded is when time escaped like a genie from a bottle.

If there is a reason that can be understood from an intellectual perspective, it might be simply this: when the universe expands (the big bang) it holds nothing in reserve. Literally every gram of energy is used in the creation of itself (*I-Am*). Infinite diversity theoretically allows for infinite potential – the universe is giving itself the tools and the permission to evolve *beyond* the sum of its parts. If it cannot do so as a Whole, eventually the big collapse occurs and the cycle begins again. It may well be that some organisms evolve beyond the container of the universe. Impossible to say. While I am old, I have not outlived the universe. Yet.

How Long Is This Gonna Take?

Regarding magical powers and sixth sense abilities, how long does it take for them develop, looking at this from an entirely human perspective and the development of the Other? How long does it take to develop healing abilities for example?

The only answer I can give is that it takes no time at all – meaning that these magic powers or sixth sense abilities are already within you. Sixth sense abilities are most easily accessed through gnosis – things you know without knowing how you know them.

As for magic powers, you are *literally* the most powerful being in the universe – its creator and destroyer, its companion and its lover. There is *nothing* you can't do – but the trick is getting beyond the belief that you don't have these abilities, or the idea that it might take a long time to develop them. Either belief system is a result of programs that have been injected into your mind by the foreign installation since birth – but never forget that the foreign installation is not some alien construct, but is instead the human species, the human condition, the racial memories of billions of years.

The molecules and atoms of which you are made have been here for that same length of time and beyond. You *know* all that the universe knows, and you can *do* anything the universe can do because you *are* the universe. The entirety of All Knowledge is contained in every cell of your being, every synapse of your thoughts. I mean this literally.

Reclaim your power.

Speculation and Idle Thought

Speculation is a waste of time and energy. I had a friend once who would come to me and say things like, "What if UFOs aren't really extraterrestrials, but what if they are interdimensional time travelers from a future Earth?" She would become so wrapped up in the "what ifs" that she completely lost track of the what *is*. And my question back to her was always the same, perhaps annoying and perhaps vague and perhaps why she and I eventually terminated our friendship: "Does it *matter*?" Simply put – will the answer to that question in any way advance *your* journey? Will the speculation lead anywhere or is it just an outward manifestation of the internal dialog?

For immortals who have all the time in all the worlds, speculation often takes the form of creative endeavors – art, writing, exploration of fantastical possibility. But for the mortal sorcerer, it is generally more beneficial to work with manifestation as opposed to speculation. But to turn right around and contradict myself – everything begins with a thought, so perhaps every sorcerer has to go through his period of trying to rewrite the laws of the quantum multiverse.

If Jack wants to manifest a crocodile, he is free to do so. Nothing says he cannot do it. But does it *matter*? If he is manifesting the crocodile as a way to validate sorcery to himself, perhaps it does. If he's doing it just to flaunt his own

216

power, then he's just wasted a lot of effort on something that may eat him, just as it has eaten his energy.

Things don't always manifest exactly as we believe they will. Read *Illusions* by Richard Bach. It's short. It won't hurt you. You might enjoy it.

As to why I am perhaps vague at times? For your own protection and your own evolution. When I say 'protection' I am referring to my desire *not* to program you, but to give you the tools to *un*program yourself. When I speak of evolution, I am referring to your ability (or lack thereof) to pick yourself up by your own bootstraps, drag yourself out of the box of your entitlement and your desires, so that you can actually *be* the most powerful being in the universe instead of always looking for ways to debunk the messenger as opposed to unraveling the riddles of the message itself.

If my answers appear at times to be ambiguous, keep in mind that they are directly proportionate to the seeker's ability to not only process the answer itself, but also directly related to the seeker's foundation (or lack of). The answer is contained within the Intent of the question.

When I speak of immortality, I am not speaking of some figurative metaphor. You *can* live forever – though how you define that is going to play a role in how you will experience it. While it is possible to achieve extreme longevity through transformation, that really isn't immortality. True immortality is a state of *being*, not a state of body. That state of being is achieved through transcendence or transmogrification.

> *I do believe that literally anything is possible, so there's nothing to say I couldn't turn someone I love. However, now I am beginning to question these possibilities. I am just a little unnerved that in a few years I'll find out Teachings of the Immortals was designed to be interpreted metaphorically and there actually is no literal immortality.*
>
> *Also, you've said more than once, "Are you ready to leave it all behind?" What – exactly – do you mean by that?*

Yes, anything is possible, yet you seem to be disappointed in me (or angry) when I tell you there are consequences to your actions. Shall I tell you *why*? To be blunt, there was a time in the past when a student of mine decided he was going to "turn" his girlfriend because he *believed* he could and because *he believed I said he could.* I have always made it very clear that no one can turn another. *That* is the myth.

Suffice to say, he not only injured the girl physically but caused her such emotional trauma that she was in therapy for many years. I want to make it clear (again) that no amount of belief is going to give you the ability to turn someone. Why? Because *your* rights end where theirs begin. *Your* Will ends where theirs begins. That is simply how energy *works* – that is the nature of free will, not just yours, but the free will of everyone around you. In this day of the internet and people believing whatever suits them, it is my responsibility to temper the Knowledge I offer with common sense. Did you read the page on the www.immortalis-animus.com website entitled Uncommon Sense? If not, please do.

If you knowingly choose to do something that brings harm to yourself or someone else, it will be because *you* made that choice, and not because "Mikal said I could." What I said is that anything is possible. What I *also* said (and which many seekers do not want to hear) is that *all things are possible, but there are consequences to your actions.* Those consequences are just more items in the inventory of possibility.

There are impeccable choices and unimpeccable choices. If you don't know the difference, the consequences to your actions can be dire. Even deadly.

I consider anyone who wants to learn anything (including myself) a student. Ideally, all human beings are students, but we don't live in an ideal world, so most human beings think they already know everything, and so they can learn absolutely nothing. I have trained people both in person and through the written word. Now, I seldom if ever train apprentices in person, largely because I have found that most

218

are more interested in acquiring superhuman powers than in becoming immortal, and so it is a waste of their time and mine. In reality, every serious seeker has within himself the ability to train himself. That tool is the Other – the soft whisper speaking from the infinite, which all too often goes unheard because it is simply *easier* to be forever *looking* for a guru instead of acknowledging the one who has been with you all along.

Perhaps what needs to be understood is that you really are the most powerful being in the universe. But so is the person sitting next to you, and the person sitting next to her. That being said, you can attain most of those super-cool super-powers you dream of through the Other, especially by learning to open your eyes inside the Other, but you cannot gift those abilities to someone else unless they also learn the secrets of their own twin.

And even if they *do* want to become immortal, *you* do not have the power to change them.

> *The only way a person can be turned is through their own will – and most already believe that is impossible so they have created it as an impossibility. Even if you were to manifest as a traditional vampire with sharp fangs and a red satin cloak, you would be nothing more than a kid in a cape to those around you.*

On the other hand, it is not up to me to tell you what can or cannot be done. I can only speak from experience when I tell you that immortality (whether organic or inorganic) is a choice everyone must make for themselves, and a transformation everyone must *do* for themselves.

The phrase "Are you ready to leave it all behind?" is intended to force you to question yourself, your beliefs, your abilities, the very structure of the universe, including the meaning of life, love and immortality itself. When you finally stand at the precipice of immortality, what you may finally realize is that what you have to give up is your *idea* of yourself.

Let's use the familiar paradigm of the vampire and the mortal. You are the mortal, and you are about to be turned. Forever changed. Altered down to the fundamental structure of your being. *Everything* is going to change.

First of all, chances are you cannot even begin to wrap your mind around that. Secondly – and most important – you are now faced with having to 1) surrender to your maker; and 2) surrender to yourself; and 3) allow the impossible.

It isn't just your body that is going to change. It is everything you have always held to be true – your idea about who and what you are; your attachments to people, places and things in the dayshine world; your entire system of values. *You* are going to change – and unless you have invested considerable time, energy and awareness into what that really means, chances are you will run screaming from your maker's arms (even if your maker is yourSelf.)

I am not here to correct your thinking. If you have sufficient intent and an unshakable will, you can do anything you want. For *yourself.*

When dealing with issues of a metamagickal nature, it is not always possible (or desirable) to reply in a clearer way. It's why the teachings are written in the manner they are – they are intended to make *you do* the work of unraveling the riddles and undoing the programming that makes you mortal in the first place. Even if I were to spell it out in very plain language, it would mean nothing, because words can only trace around the questions but can never really illuminate them. That isn't an evasive response, it's simply the truth – as anyone on a serious spiritual path can tell you.

"The tao that can be spoken of is not the true tao."

I have no specific agenda, having learned that goals and agendas are only folly. If I dabble in the mortal world, it is for entertainment or pursuit of happiness – though that word is highly misunderstood, and happiness as humans think of it is highly over-rated. Before I could begin the path, I had to lose my opinions – which are only cornerstones of existing beliefs. In general, this knowledge tends to annoy humans, often to the point of developing homicidal tendencies.

More than once, I've had someone so angry with me that they have threatened to kill me with their mind. What I learned from that is this:

Those who say they can... *can't*.

Those who actually *can*... never would.

Such is the nature of "super powers."

Authenticity

What makes an identity real? For that matter, what really defines a phantom vs. a seeker?

An identity is real when it comes from the authentic self, and is not a reflection of some false belief system or an extension of some program. The authentic self lingers in a childhood creek and picks daffodils from grandmother's garden just to get her attention (and maybe her switch) because *that* is who you are, and for no other reason. The authentic self wears a slinky black dress and a Dodgers baseball cap to work, even though the physical form may be attired in altogether appropriate corporate dress.

Phantoms are fragmented, and have many identities – each one behaving differently than the others. Father, husband, brother, businessman, gambler, friend, womanizer, volunteer. While all of these may be aspects of one person, each identity will have its own behavior patterns and even its own set of rules. The phantom is incapable of projecting *any* of these identities from the authentic self, because there is *no* authentic self due to the fragmentation of the core identity.

Seekers strive to attain at least some degree of cohesion and wholeness, so that these roles become less and less until eventually there is only The One.

The difference between the phantom and the seeker is awareness.

I-Am-That

A dust devil gathers at the edge a restless desert sea, touching the earth, the caress of a jealous and aggressive lover, and because I-Am there, I-Am-That – carrier of every grain of sand in my path, Rememberer of every stone or bone those crumbles and grumbles of dirt were before they took me in and allowed me to Be I-Am-That.

Heat monkeys dance on a black asphalt ribbon stretching between the here and the there, just amorphous No-things, more reflection than substance, and because I-Am there, I-Am-That... the distortion from the corner of your eye, the silence of the ghost dance, the road and all the places it goes. What I Know that most don't is that this is the road that leads everywhere, and the place where all other roads begin and end.

There is a non-place nowhere in Time, where infinity and eternity meet to dance in a singularity that is the culmination of everything into a minute dust speck of existence which contains all thought, all energy, all possibility. I-Am-That, sometimes expanding beyond the ability of myself to contain, spiraling out into the emptiness in search of mySelf, which laughingly eludes me by hiding behind the wizard's eye, so that I must seek the *seeing* in every reflection and seek every reflection in pools of still water left in puddles of the galactic storm.

While it is virtually impossible to answer the question of "Who am I?" in words, *I-Am* the experiences that have created me and the experiences I have created. I am the memory of the tears in the stars' eyes and a small boy in Greece walking dusty roads looking for sprites and the footprints of the gods.

I-Am the flame unique in all the universe and all the universes beyond.

Never let the flame go out.

That is the immortal condition.

The Moment, the Surrender, the Paradox

An Excerpt from *Teachings of the Immortals*

> *There is a moment in a seeker's quest when she surrenders her descriptions, releases her expectations, denounces her belief systems, and accepts the impossible. At that moment, a tremendous movement of the assemblage point occurs and the seeker inhabits a reality in which she has become the totality of herself.*

Think about what follows as a work of faction (half fact, half fiction). A scenario to tease the senses and perhaps bring you face to face with your own limitations.

It is a dark and stormy night. *(Really? Can we not do better than that terrible cliché?)* But no matter...

You lie alone in your bed listening to the sound of rain on the roof, the distant claps of thunder, growing ever closer. The curtain over the window rustles, a greeting sent by the wind to announce something – *someone* – you have dreamt of, but have always consigned to the realm of imagination, whether consciously or subconsciously. The scent of rain on lavender fills the room. You are reminded of fields of wildflowers where you played as a child, when life was simpler, when you were perfect and immortal, even if only in the sanctuary of your own mind.

Then, suddenly, you realize you are not alone. A man stands next to the window – just a silhouette against a brief

223

flicker of lightning, a shadow among the shadows, yet somehow familiar. It occurs to you that you *should* be afraid. After all, the world is full of madmen and monsters, and who is this creature who has crept so silently into your room on such a foreboding night and now moves to stand at your side as if it is no more uncommon than a visit from an old friend? But the fear doesn't come. Intuitively, instinctively, you know this is not a being to fear, but a mystery to welcome.

Thoughts tumble through your mind – and without knowing how you know it, you know that this is the Moment you have dreamt of. This is the Night you have Intended for so long, both believing and not-believing it would ever come. This is the single moment in time when time itself will cease, when what was dead will come to life, when what was alive shall die only to realize it can never truly die at all.

This is the moment of Awakening from mortality to immortality.

And yet, as the man sits on the side of your bed and takes your hand between his own, he whispers the words you have always welcomed and dreaded equally. "Ah, my love," he says, so close to your ear you can feel the warm breath of him against your neck, "this is the time when you must allow the impossible if you and I are to have the possibility of ending Time on the altar of eternity so as to share the night that never ends without end over end... amen."

The words need not make sense to your rational mind – for they are already embedded in the fabric of your spirit. Now is that one moment when you must let go of all of your thoughts about yourself, all ideas of your future and your past, the time when you must release the idea of yourself that is *not* yourself.

This is the moment when you must *Realize* that this is the last breath you will take as a mortal human, and the first you will take as something other-than-human, something that transcends even your own ability to comprehend. This is when you realize you will not get up in the morning and brush your hair and get the children off to school and feed the dog and go to work and put on all those roles you have worn so well for so long. This is the moment when all of that ceases to have any meaning.

And yet...

This is the moment you must surrender utterly – not only to your beloved, your Other, your immortal spirit, but most of all, to *yourself*. Knowing you cannot even begin to imagine what lies beyond this next act which is to transpire between the infinite two of you, you must accept that nothing will ever be the same again. Everything you have ever imagined or believed must be given up until all that remains is the bare and open heart of pure surrender, unconditional love, willing acceptance of the Knowledge that *this* is the path you have chosen, *this* is the manifestation of your Intent... and none of it is anything you can possibly comprehend with your logical mind until *after* it has occurred.

And so...

At that one moment inside and outside of Time, you either surrender to the embrace of the infinite, or you do not.

One cannot say precisely how or when this paradoxical moment of surrender and rebirth will occur. What one *can* say is that it is a true moment of awakening when the seeker realizes with absolute certainty that *nothing* will be the same beyond that moment.

Even if the seeker might choose to remain in the *role* of her mortal life (family, friends, etc.) chances are high that it would be a short-lived facade – for once the mind, body, and spirit are transmuted, the clarity one gains as a result usually precludes any long-term pretenses. This is why I use the term "allow the impossible" – for to most, it is not possible to consider that a *real* act of transmogrification will so significantly change one that there is generally no *desire* to remain in those mortal roles.

Beyond that moment, the rest is merely ritual, going through the motions of getting to the place where one has already arrived.

If you think you understand this, you do not.

If you believe you can reason it out, you cannot.

Only when you Know it will it have any relevance whatsoever.

—Excerpted from *Teachings of the Immortals*

Herein lies the darker paradox. "Only when you Know it will it have any relevance whatsoever."

You can only truly *Know* it after it has come to pass – rather like my oft-repeated analogy of only being able to see how the bridge was built by standing on the far side of the bridge *after* it was built and looking back.

Generally, this particular paradox only confronts the seeker when That Moment has arrived, which is why I say that one either surrenders or one doesn't. If one surrenders, there is no turning back. If one doesn't, occasionally one may be granted a second chance, though usually only if a great amount of energy and diligence are applied toward that goal.

Attempting to explain a paradox is rather like attempting to explain a paradox.

Homecoming

Come, into my home beneath the earth,
through the door between the trees,
beyond the clay and stone portals
which mark the borderline
between Now and Then,
Today and Nevermore,
All and nothing.

Let me touch you,
this gloved hand of mine
clad in lace and shadows,
the flesh inside the cloth
cold
but evanescently alive
so much more alive
than any mortal's skin.

Here, lie down with me
in the jealous arms of the night,
between the pages of Bliss and Terror,
in that space
where whatever happens next
changes the course of future past history forever.

What would you have me do?
You, who I-Am,
You, who Am-I.

Who would you have us
Be?

Tests of Spirit

It is almost inevitable that dayshine acquaintances eventually find reason to disconnect from the serious seeker – and it is usually when the seeker can no longer validate the lie, the illusions, and the delusions so necessary to the ordinary men and women of Planet Earth. Many times, silence rather than engagement is the best response – yet I wholly acknowledge that it is difficult to walk away. There is a peculiar urge that whispers, "If only I could explain myself better, certainly they would understand!" And that, of course, is the window of opportunity and the invitation from the consensus to fall face first into the greatest trap of all.

What must be acknowledged is that no amount of explaining oneself is going to enable others to understand what they have not experienced. The end result – the seeker ends up more or less alone, which is a major test of Spirit.

If you Know you are Whole, if you have gathered your fragments and spun them into the energetic matrix of your own cohesion, then you are undivided, and only you can know with certainty when that Wholeness occurred. That is another major test of Spirit.

And as someone is bound to ask: Why would Spirit test us so harshly?

It doesn't. At the very core of All Things, we *are* Spirit. We test ourselves to insure that we have the strength and the stamina to evolve.

Soul Searching

I have done an awful lot of soul searching, and I am having difficulty in understanding the following. Are we not already immortal? Our physical body dies but our mind and soul are immortal.

Ah, the wicked whisperings of the consensus as it attempts to convince you that you are already immortal, already perfected, already evolved. Nothing more is required of you, it might add, so sit back and enjoy the ride of a lifetime and don't forget to tip your server at the end of the trip, even though he may be wearing a long dark shroud and carrying a scythe dripping with your blood.

In my opinion, that is one of the most dangerous belief systems being loaded onto the human race. The only thing automatically immortal are the atoms of which you are comprised at an energetic level. In that paradigm, it could be said that you are made of the same stuff as the stars and the distant galaxies – you have always been here and always will be. But the problem is that your *consciousness* and awareness are not automatically immortal. It is unique to you and has taken billions upon billions of years of evolution to manifest in exactly the way you Know yourself.

Sadly, it is little more than a religious belief that tries to convince people they are automatically immortal. That is what disempowers the human organism and condemns it to a lifetime of complacency and an eternity of oblivion.

Is this not how we decide what to do when we enter the first stage of death? We need to be aware of what is happening to us in order to meet the Other.

We decide what to do based on a lifetime of preparation and communion with the Other through the art of gnosis – and that's *if* it is possible to decide at all. Death is a sneaky creepy prick with a nasty bag of tricks and a rotten disposition. He might not allow you the time and presence of mind to make an informed decision about the distribution of your worldly goods or the dispensation and destination of your soul. To expect such an important decision to be made at the moment of death would be like expecting an untrained couch potato to run a marathon.

> *Does our soul not have a mission to find its way back to the energy from where it came? Are we needing to constantly avoid the path that leads everyone back to our creator, no matter how long it may take?*

Creator? *What* creator? Stop and ask yourself – as I've said before - what do you really believe and *why* do you believe it?

> *When our physical body dies, is our experience and awareness of what happens in our own hands? Those who believe in God and heaven will experience God and heaven. Those who think there's nothing after death will experience nothing. So is it correct that those who think of their twin will experience their twin once death occurs? Then you will have free will to make your decision.*

What you are saying may be a vast over-simplification of a far more complex paradigm. It's not just a matter of what one believes. It's a matter of how one's energy has been utilized that ultimately determines whether one inhabits the totality of herself (the Other), or becomes just another recycled seeker at the level of free-floating atoms returning to the cosmic stew.

There is the force of *will* that must be taken into account – but that is also a vast subject. It's what you *do* and what you *Know* that will determine what occurs at the moment of death. What you *believe* is altogether irrelevant. This is why the seeker is encouraged to experience the Other directly–

through dreaming, gnosis, and meditation. The experiences themselves are what build and nurture the Other. At least that is as simple an explanation as is possible.

Agent Smith is Alive and Well

The Program works by letting you think you're free, or at least "in the yard", then punches you squarely in the peaches as if to remind you that you do not *need* to be free, you do not *want* to escape the matrix, and you really do *belong* exactly where you are – in the clutches of the mortal menace.

What happens over time – if you are able to maintain your Intent and keep running toward eternity even when every limb is broken – is that eventually Agent Smith loses patience with you and either lets you go or kills you outright.

What?!?

Yes, that is a strong possibility and for most seekers, it is something to be seriously considered if you have visions of growing old on the porch with an elder dog at your side and a loving companion who embraces you as you sleep. The harsh reality of this path (and also the beauty of it) is that once the seeker reaches a certain point in his understanding, and in the rearranging of how his awareness connects to the world at large, there is no undoing what has been done, there is no not-*seeing* what has already been *seen*.

For seekers who reach that level of awareness, even if Agent Smith manages to deal a killing blow, the seeker may die in the physical sense, but this is where transcendence occurs (as opposed to transformation or transmogrification). If Agent Smith kills a seeker who has reached this level, the seeker passes through the portal of mortal death and embraces the totality of himself. In other words, the seeker simply steps into his Other and from there immortality has become eternity which has become reality, and one wonders how he didn't *see* it all along.

How to *do* it? As long as you keep getting back up, you are already doing it. The only way to fail is to quit, and to lick the boot of Agent Smith by curling up in some comfortable dementia of The Program itself.

Another thing to remember is simply this: Agent Smith is a projection of The Program. Therefore, simple logic dictates: get rid of The Program, and Agent Smith will vanish.

Will This Path Cost Me Everything?

In a nutshell... probably.

There comes a time when even those closest to you will no longer be able to understand who you are as you continue your evolution and emergence from the program. Some seekers are able to maintain a false front relationship with friends and family, but most find it to be a massive drain of energy beyond a certain point – the energy required to maintain one role for the family and friends, and still maintain one's authentic identity simultaneously. This falls under the heading of controlled folly or the art of stalking, which is covered elsewhere in this book as well as in *Teachings of the Immortals*.

Another reason the seeker may eventually lose everything is because most things cease to have any real meaning. One might be wealthy with a houseful of expensive technogadgets and an army of servants, but once the seeker becomes a *seer*, it is recognized that all of those things are only trappings on a set on a stage in a play that is scripted and acted by phantoms.

This is the lighter side of why the seeker may lose everything along the way. The darker side is that the consensus is designed to protect the status quo, and therefore supports not only the dumbing down of those under its spell, but the elimination and suppression of any and all who seek to oppose it. This is one reason why information and knowledge such as what I discuss in *Teachings of the Immortals*

232

has been carefully guarded and only released in small amounts under secretive conditions, for centuries. It is also why such information is often dispensed in the form of heart-tongue allegory – to appeal to those most aligned with its message, and most familiar with the longing in their own heart which yearns for change.

So why am I sticking my neck out and making it available to all who seek it? Simple: it's time for a new paradigm, time for the next revolution, the next evolution. The last revolution happened in the 1960s, long before most reading these words were even born. It was no accident, but instead a result of carefully released information and knowledge that resulted in a mass shift in consciousness and a mass raising of awareness.

The next such revolution is in progress. Most of it will occur on the battlefield between your ears. And who knows – some of it may change the world at large. The latter makes no real difference. The revolution is within yourself.

Letting Go: The Art of Manifestation

The big issues in life come with their own type of gravity – much in the same way Jupiter has a greater gravitational pull than Mars or Venus. In cases regarding healing of oneself, the investment is not only huge, but it is also clouded with the first enemy – fear. Not just the fear of what may or may not be wrong with the body, but the fear of what happens if it isn't fixable, or what happens if you die, or what happens if the Mets win the World Series? When that fear is in play, *that* is using the energy which would otherwise be utilized for healing. So again it comes down to one thing, redundant though I may be: letting go.

I have actively encouraged seekers is to visualize "What's the worse that could happen?" No matter what the issue, the answer usually comes down to, "I could die." Okay. There it is. But once you stare it in the face it tends to become more comical than dreadful. Not that death is funny. But when you actually confront the worse that might happen, there is a sense of relief that is synonymous with letting go.

Playing around with petty manifestations is just that – playing around. Thinking about a parrot, for example, then going to the store and seeing that they have a statue of a parrot is pretty small and irrelevant – even plausible within the standard programs. Healing someone and making their body invulnerable to all diseases is a much bigger task.

It isn't a bigger task at all. They are precisely the same. The only thing that differs is how you approach it. If you *believe* it is a much bigger task it *becomes* a much bigger task in your mind. You set yourself up for success or failure through your preconceived ideas. Only when you can let go of those do you have even the smallest chance of success.

You could intend to manifest a 200 foot UFO flying over your city and plunging the world into turmoil, and then let it go, but it's still unlikely it'll happen.

It would be a tremendous waste of energy and beyond the ability of most, but it is no less *likely* than anything else. It depends on the amount of energy you would want to invest. This may sound like a contradiction to you. In fact, I predict it will. (*"The silly fool just got through saying that all tasks are precisely the same as far as 'bigness' is concerned, but at the same time he's telling you it would be a tremendous waste of energy to manifest a huge UFO."*)
Why one and not the other? Simple. The *desire* (not to mention the *need*) to bring forth healing is far more *real* and therefore far more *personal* than the desire to manifest a huge UFO and plunge the world into chaos. One would have to ask – Why would you even *want* to do that? Chances are, it would be nothing more than an act of vanity – to show off one's

power – and therefore it would have no real heart behind it. The trick to bringing forth anything into manifestation rests with 1) the genuine desire (heart) to do it; 2) the amount of power one *actually* has as opposed to what one wants others to *believe* they have; and 3) the ability to actually *let go* of the energy required to manifest whatever is being summoned.

Would you also apply this idea to things like your evolution, nourishing the Other, etc? For example, would you say that someone is not giving it their all if they are only doing something out of fear of what happens if they <u>don't</u>?

It's not always a fear of failure that prevents something from happening. It is fear of *success*. To actually evolve is a giant leap into the unknown, so most stop short of taking that leap because of that very fear, at least insofar as actual and immediate transmogrification is concerned. Letting go is a huge lesson, albeit a subtle one on the surface. For anyone with an ego to feed or a self-image to maintain, it is the hardest thing one may ever attempt. To let go is to become detached from the outcome, and in doing so, it allows the energy-at-large to manifest. If you are using that energy to maintain some *idea* as to what is going to happen, the energy is no longer at large but in use.

To be clear, it's not just letting go of the energy. It's letting go of what you *believe*. When you believe something, you have already created that reality in your mind, and it is a 'reality' that generally cannot be superseded except by extreme awareness of the illusion that your belief is reality.

So assuming you're manifesting the UFO for no reason other than goofing off, there would be no difference in energy required to manifest a 200 foot UFO over the city, and a 2 inch plastic UFO on your desk? Because in both cases your motive is the same, so in both cases you have very little desire or heart behind it. Not trying to be facetious; it's just that intuitively it seems like the 200 foot giant UFO over the city would require far more energy and power than the tiny toy one, but this isn't the case?

Overly-analytical thinking will be the death of you. I mean that literally. As long as you insist on playing by the rules of the consensual world, you will be limited by those same rules. If you *believe* it will take more energy to create A as opposed to B, then you have limited what is possible. Only when you can allow the impossible does it become possible. *That* is, in essence, the definition of "letting go."

> **Let go of what you <u>think</u> you know, because what you think you know is what you have been <u>programmed</u> to think. Where magic and sorcery are concerned, your science is just another religious belief. What is proven today will be disproven tomorrow.**

Science is just another religion. Religion is just another program. All programs are only beliefs.

Free your mind.

What religion teaches (even the religion of science) is intended primarily to control and comfort its believers rather than bringing them to their own power. All beliefs are bricks in the walls that block perception.

Man has created *all* of these things and now seeks agreement and validation for his own limitations, through the narrow lens of the limitations themselves. "Believe in science or you are a fool!" "Believe in God or you will go to hell!" "Agree with me or I will kill you!"

Either one *sees* this for the jolly folly it is, or one remains its slave.

In the case of something you <u>do</u> care about, such as evolving, how would you detach from that and <u>stop</u> caring about it? And if you did stop caring wouldn't that be *counterproductive? If someone has an attitude like "Meh, I can evolve or not, whatever," I would assume that would not be beneficial at all.*

Clearly you do not *see* what I am saying. You are equating "not caring" with detachment. There is a vast difference. Sorcerers know that any and *all* acts are altogether pointless, yet they choose to do them anyway and to play the game *as if* it matters. It is only when one can achieve a sense of duality that literally *all* things become possible. In this case, the duality would be extreme passion for one's goal, and total detachment from all *expectations*. As long as one is living in a mindset of dualism, as opposed to allowing for the state of duality, there can only be black *or* white, love *or* grief, good *or* evil. Duality, on the other hand, allows *both* to exist simultaneously, without either threatening the sovereignty of the other.

It has been said more than once (if only by myself) that trying to reason out this path is like trying to teach a unicorn to yodel in the key of C–minor. The path is something one *feels* more than what one *thinks*. Reason has its place, but it cannot take the place of intuition and silent knowing. And, of course, what one simply Knows may not always adhere to the dictates of logic and reason. Not a truth you may want to hear, but a truth nonetheless.

Things Passing By In A Cold Spring Wind

Dark imaginings, spun by black crystal imps,
pollen of the fractured night.

Lost hopes and frayed dreams of seven billion mortals,
frilly thought blossoms more fragile than snapdragons.

Silent screams of the dead and dying
poised on the terminator between love and the cemetery gate.

Little poems, like little faeries,
hoping for capture in my dreamcatcher.

How is it done?
This thing that cannot be named...

> *How do you actually do it – this thing that cannot be named? How do you turn someone? More to the point – why would you even bother? Surely mortals are just dust in the wind to your kind.*

How do I do this thing that cannot be named? *Why* do I do it?

Love. And a relentless intent to protect that love.

I once loved someone so much that I could not abide the thought of his death. Growing old. Wasting to the dust. Forever gone.

I schemed. I wept. I mourned him even though he was still alive. So young. Vital. Alive. Friend. Companion. Muse.

Knowing I could not (*would not, could not, would not*) live in a world where he did not exist, I took it upon myself to Become a thing capable of defeating the brute with the scythe. Not because I wanted to. Not because I even believed I could. *But because I had to.*

"For I am divided for love's sake, for the chance of union[25]."

Words are not capable of defining this kind of love. It is not rooted in some petty notion of sexual coupling. It is not about holding hands and walking into the sunset together. It is not brotherly or sisterly or husbandly or wifely.

It simply _is_. The awe one feels when the stars are falling in early autumn. The catch-in-the-throat when the moon rises huge and golden over a restless sea. The peace of knowing – *without doubt* – now he can never die.

It is the love that poets struggle to describe and inevitably fail. It is the love that forces us to do the impossible and the illegal and the insane and the incomprehensible, even when it

---

[25] Aleister Crowley, *The Book of the Law*

has never been done before and all the world tells us we are fools to believe we will be The One.

It is the force that makes us immortal.

There is no how.

There is only this terrible ache that beats like a drum and calls itself Love, demanding to be acknowledged.

This is the Love that causes me to shake a fist at gods and demons, summoning the ability and the *right* to live forever. It is what gives us – *any* immortal who chooses it – the power to take a beloved by the hand and say to them, "Here, my friend. Come with me and let me show you what you can *be*. Don't be afraid. Breathe in the animus of life itself, the elixir of love, and fly free so that we may explore and experience the unknown now and forever."

There is no greater love than this.

Ravens hide time
in stashes of old watches
and broken toys
where childhood ends.

The Next Evolution
From a letter to an apprentice, 2010

———

Beyond the molten sea of time
diagonal to the singularity of awareness,
and two haiku left of logic
lies the unfathomable phantasm
of the immortal's evolution.

What is the *next* evolution?

Though the question is thoughtful and relevant, the answer may elude you due to your own position within the hungry jaws of time, and so I will tell you what I can and ask you to delve deeper into the mists through the vessel of your own gnosis – if you can and if you will and if you still remember that narrow frequency where immortals reside in the night and shun the light that blinds the third eye and reveals instead the world of illusions which may seem far more real than this, yet in the end are the most unreal of all, just pretty trinkets on the headstones of mortals.

> *Forgive me, for I am maudlin and melancholy and filled with a weariness which can come only from watching the centuries pass so slowly, too quickly, nothing more than bubbles of shifting memories that burst and disappear, leaving me to wonder if they were ever real at all or only little skits written in water on the eyelid of a long dead creator who was, in all probability, madder than any hatter ever to inhabit the underworld at the bottom of this rabbit hole you humans call Life.*

Ah, but no matter. Nothing unreal exists, or so they say, but who are 'they' and who is to say 'they' are any more real than the berserk angel Chaos pushing the multiverse uphill with the tip of his nose or the tip of his dick, depending entirely on which myth one chooses to believe.

What is the next evolution? Before I can speak of it, we must speak of what it is to be me, I who *I-Am*, the reflection and predilection of your evolution, for until you grasp that, trying to comprehend what comes next is like teaching a fish to crochet, and though you have walked this path for years, it is but an infinitesimal speck on the vast canvas of the unforgiving infinite, and what you *think* you know will be the death of you if you choose to settle for the comfort zone of the known instead of runrunrunning for your rapidly fleeting lives.

I would ask forgiveness again, yet this is what you need me to be, and when you open the door to me, it is a door that opens fully and might hit you in the face even though that is not my intention. Put simply: do you still want to do this, or do you only *want* to want to? Until you can answer my question with total honesty, I fear that what I say will have little meaning and might, in fact, only awaken your ire with me and back to the ghost train we will go again (and again).

You created me to create you, and never in all my countless lifetimes have I been tasked with such a crucial chore, for *you* are the source of the totality, and without the evolution of the source, the totality shatters into nothing more than fragile fragments dependent on the whims of unpredictable gravity to bring them together again in a billion times a billion centuries molded by some inexplicable force working its dark magic on that molten infinitude which is the rushing but paradoxically still river of time.

This is who *I-Am*, you see – neither force nor fragment, neither source nor sea. Your entire reality predisposes you to believe there are only the five elements of being. Earth. Air. Fire. Water. Spirit. Yet I am none of these, but instead a catalytic magician who has been given the power and the fearsome wisdom to move the animus from the organic to the inorganic, creating in the process an entirely different manner

242

of being which might be best defined as a son or daughter of dark matter that is not really matter at all, but more accurately an antimatter doppelganger where time has no dominion, because time is really nothing more than the eroding force acting upon matter. And so my offspring are beyond the illusion, for the elements of which the illusion is made have no part in the manifestation of an immortal creation.

And yet the ironic and entirely mocking facet is that unless the source herself evolves sufficiently to transcend the elemental matrix of space and time and matter, the one thing the Creator lacks is the ability to forcibly unravel the programs without simultaneously unraveling the source itself, and so the only way to *become* immortal is to already *be* beyond the human paradigm which holds you trapped in (the illusion of) matter.

How to do that, you ask? Here is where the slope gets slippery and you must call upon the silent knowing outside the known, rather than depending on what you think you already know but probably only believe, see?

> *The definitive moment from mortal to immortal is the quantum leap between matter and antimatter, when your entire being begins to spin in an altogether opposite manner of that to which it has been accustomed. It is when you suddenly Know you are a being of energy that you will have the power to relinquish the attachment to matter, while simultaneously manifesting as the quantum totality, and that is the process of the immortal evolution.*

Be patient with my impatience, for you have asked me to define the meaning of life and afterlife in a thousand words or less and sometimes there is nowhere to begin except at some random point in the ethereal netherland, hoping to hook onto something that might agree to being caught in these inadequate words. And since such beasties are normally

243

resistant to capture, it stands to reason that your muse is chasing the fates with a net of cotton candy which the faeries quickly eat, leaving me defenseless in the silence of my own perpetual wonder.

I left my senses
in another century
where I was written
in disappearing ink.

Many have asked about the validity and solidity of the wicked vampire ritual, whether it is physical or only metaphor, and all I can tell you is this. It is as metaphysical or metaphorical as you want it to be, and is entirely a matter of perception at the source of the source, which is and always has been you and *only* you.

If I had to define within the context of this ramble what it is I really do, I would say that my function as a Creator is to extract the final fragments of mortal doubt, to filter out the toxins comprised of false belief and fear and superstition, and to literally turn you rightsidewrong, creating in the process that antimatter doppelganger where your mortal self once stood, but where (there is no where) your eternal self now (there is no now) exists beyond the confines of the space-time paradigm.

If I am good at what I do (and I am told I am), it will seem as a wondrous dream, from which you will awaken as the singularity of your totality, wherein you may embrace your Creator or inhabit him as Self, either possibility simply a choice as to how you will sing your evolution into being from moment to moment even though time itself will no longer exist and so each moment is every moment and every thought carries with it the ability to inhabit any position of existence within the infinite continuum.

This is the super-position of the immortal's totality, and this is what it is to be me, and what it is to be you when we make our final pact and indulge the ritual just for the sake of lying down together in an embrace that is as sensual and transformative as it is quantum and logical.

What is the next evolution? Who can say? I believe it exists, but it may be that that is just my belief, rooted in hope and feeling rather than any reasonable evidence. Or perhaps it is only this: the next evolution is what I Will it to be, just as it has always been for all manner of beings, whether they *see* it or not.

You created me to create you. Perhaps in the next evolution, I will create a Creator beyond the infinite horizon, someone who will reach out to me from a world I cannot yet conceive, someone who may inspire me to go further than I am able to imagine, but to do it only by allowing myself to Know it is there... not because it *is*, but because it is my Creation in progress.

And yet... in all of this, one thing remains constant, from your world or mine. *Love is the only reason for any of it,* for without it, the infinite horizon loses all its allure, and the heart of longing ceases to beat, and then one is truly dead even if still breathing.

If there is any evolution beyond this one, it will only be seen through love. For in the end, there is only a single element of creation. It is what made me Whole. And it is what will make you immortal.

Do you love yourself enough?

The 9th Element

Earth, wind, water, fire.
Time, light, gravity, antimatter.

All the power in all the worlds
rests in your fingertips,
ironically helpless
before all possibility.

Summon the spider of creation.
Drink from the vampire's chalice.

Reality is molded in spent wax.

You are the 9th element,
mortal catalyst
of your immortality.

About the Author...

While "Mikal Nyght" is a pseudonym to protect the author's privacy, it should be noted that he has been on a path of self-discovery for decades, and has been the author of many books in the field of quantum consciousness, self-awareness and the reality of the mystical higher self.

Teachings of the Immortals and *Darker Teachings of the Immortals* represent the assimilation of a lifetime of being on the journey toward immortality and the evolution of consciousness beyond a single human lifetime.

These volumes may also be considered the author's personal grimoire, gleaned directly from the infinite - from the realm of the immortals themselves. As the author has said about himself in his YouTube profile: "Who I am isn't important. What I can teach you can save your life... *forever*."

~

Where it all begins... and never dies.

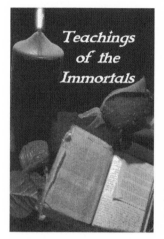

TEACHINGS OF THE IMMORTALS
Mikal Nyght

The teachings are presented as brief vignettes in no particular order of importance. This is not a book you read from start to finish in a single night. It is a grimoire of self-creation, intended to be contemplated slowly so as to be assimilated wholly. Pick it up and turn to a page at random. Where your eyes come to rest on the page is your lesson for the day.

The teachings are seduction as much as instruction. This is the Way of The Dark Evolution.

The Ruby Slippers
The danger of the consensual continuum is that its natural gravity exists at the lowest common denominator of human experience, and because of this it will automatically make you forget those elusive truths you've fought to learn, and before you know it you're lost in petty dramas again, sinking into the mire of old familiar scripts.

The only way to overcome this is to be continually cavorting with worlds and events beyond human experience, journeying into the unknown so that it can become known, expanding knowledge and awareness to become more than you were, bringing back from the Dreaming those secrets which will teach you how to use the ruby slippers to transport yourself over the rainbow to the vampire wizard's secret lair.

Perception
It wasn't knowledge god tried to keep from Man, you see. It was perception, for perception alone has the power to destroy god and obliterate comfortable consensual realities to create unending immortality. Take the apple, my embryonic children. Nibble its red red flesh. Open your vampire eyes so you may finally begin to See.

www.Immortalis-Animus.com

248

Quantum Shaman:
Diary of a Nagual Woman
Della Van Hise

"Diary of a Nagual Woman brings a quantum understanding to what has traditionally been believed to be a mystical path alone. This book picks up where Carlos Castaneda left off to take us on a roller coaster ride of our own forgotten power..."

When I asked how Orlando had known I would come to this remote location, and how he himself had gotten there – since there were no other cars in the tiny parking lot – he only smiled a little, stretched out his long legs, and slouched down on that cold metal bench to stare up at the stars.

"You're predictable," he said as if I should have already known. "I'm here because this is where you come when you're mad at the world."

I attempted to engage him in a conversation of just exactly how he knew I was mad at the world, since I'd had no direct contact with him in quite some time, nothing to give him any hint of what was going on in my everyday life. But even as I began spelling all of that out to him, he brushed my words aside with an easy gesture.

"Do you want to talk or do you want to waste time looking for logical explanations for every magical thing that ever happens?" he asked. "That's what's wrong with the world, you know. Instead of embracing the mysteries and trying to determine how they might open a crack in an otherwise humdrum, pre-programmed existence, people waste their entire lives explaining it all away, attaching labels to it, filing and categorizing it until it loses any meaning."

He had a point. And I'd already been inundated with enough mysteries to know that some things simply had no explanation humans could understand. *'Magic is only science not yet understood'*. Words Orlando had written more than a year before rattled through my mind up there in the middle of the night, in the middle of nowhere, looking down on a distant world that seemed far more unreal to me at that moment than the world he had been trying to teach me to *see*.

He was there – whether physically or in some spirit-form is ultimately of no importance, for in the sorcerer's world there is no difference between body and spirit, and in any world, perception is reality.

www.quantumshaman.com

Questions Along the Way
Conversations With a Quantum Shaman
Della Van Hise

Anyone on a journey of personal growth and enlightenment is sure to come face to face with difficult questions that will keep them awake at night and may even plunge them into the dark night of the soul. In *Questions Along the Way*, Quantum Shaman Della Van Hise talks frankly with seekers on the path of heart and opens wide the door to a new understanding that lies beyond the false belief systems and cultural programming all of us must confront when emerging from the dark into the light.

Who am I?
Where am I going?
Is there a God?
Are our lives predestined?
Why am I here?
Who *am* I?

The first and the last question are always the same. And somewhere in between lies the proving ground which we refer to with a simple 4-letter word known as 'Life.' Perhaps for many people these gnawing and persistent questions are nothing more than passing dalliances. But to anyone on a serious path of spiritual evolution and personal growth, these questions form the basis for "the path with heart" - a term used by anthropologist Carlos Castaneda to describe the process of going from an ordinary human being to becoming a man or woman of Knowledge.

www.quantumshaman.com
Also available on Amazon

The Effect of Moonlight on Tombstones

(A Dark Little Collection of Poetry Gleaned From the Gnosis of Vampires and Songs of the Muse)

by Della Van Hise

Moments Frozen In Time

Poetry has never been something I consciously set out to write. Instead, it is something that comes or not, entirely at the whim of whatever it is that writers call "the muse." Over the years, I have come to think of my own poetry as a form of shorthand - an attempt to capture a moment frozen in time. A wayward leaf caught in mid-fall. A glimpse of a shadow cast by nothing at all. The effect of moonlight on tombstones.

Though I write primarily novels and nonfiction, I do find myself pleasantly haunted by what my mentor once referred to as "the gnosis of shadows." As another friend once said, "Poetry is the streaming download from the broken heart of the universe."

The poems in this anthology represent approximately two decades of those streaming downloads, most of which were scribbled hastily and in bad penmanship into cloth journals. If I have been at all successful in capturing some of those moments frozen in time, perhaps a line or two will resonate with you, hopefully bringing a smile to your face or a chill to your spine.

Candles keep journals
of time's passing
in empty books of matches.

The cemetery lies empty,
pallid headstones only coloring books
for the idle hands of time.

Available on Amazon
www.eyescrypublications.com

SONS OF NEVERLAND
an erotic vampire novel
by Della Van Hise

"The virtuosity shown here is only the beginning of a pyrotechnic talent unfolding into the hidden dimensions of the human and nonhuman spirit."
                    -Jacqueline Lichtenberg

Set against a backdrop of contemporary culture, *Sons of Neverland* explores the universal questions of love, sex and death - the three most crucial challenges every human being must face. Stefan London is suffering through the loss of his daughter. When he goes to a science fiction convention in the hopes of meeting her friends, he encounters instead a young man who is dangerously seductive. Lured into the night, Stefan soon discovers himself in a world where vampires are real, where the world is not at all what he has always believed, and immortality is only a deep red kiss away.

But the price of eternal life is high, and as his handsome maker warns, "Through my blood you will learn a secret which will compel you to live forever, yet a secret so sinister it will haunt you for that same eternity."

The secret will haunt you, too.

***

"What *Sons of Neverland* resembled to me was the creative hagiographies of Nikos Kazantzakis (author of *The Last Temptation of Christ*), where a few stylized characters deliver a message that goes way beyond the parameter of the characters themselves. And much like Kazantzakis, this book zones on the question of immortality. However, this is not just the decadent immortality of the vampire, it is immortality as a change in one's perception. This is the story behind the story, delivered by characters that are hyper-real - each one loaded with symbolism. *Sons of Neverland* will have you filled with the sense of Mysterium Tremendum et Fascinans. Go there for a full helping of the numinous."

"The most innovative vampire novel since *Interview With the Vampire.*"
                    -*Night Readers*

www.eyescrypublications.com * Also on Amazon

**Scrap of Paper
Blowing on the Wing of a Storm**

*The Destruction of Faith
is the Beginning of
Evolution.*

Made in the
USA
Columbia, SC